Newport
Beach

Gayle Baker, Ph.D.

Other books by Gayle Baker:
  The Wet Mountain Valley, 1975
  Trial and Triumph, 1977
  Catalina Island, 2002
  Santa Barbara, 2003
  Cambria, 2003

Printed in Canada by Hignell Book Printing

Library of Congress Cataloging in Publication Data:

Baker, Gayle
      Newport Beach/Gayle Baker, Ph.D.
      1st p. cm. ed.
      Includes index.
      ISBN 0-9710984-3-3
      History of Newport Beach, California
      I. Title

      PCN 2003114784

*Cover watercolor by **Larry Iwerks**, who studied at San Francisco State University, the Mendocino Art Center, and at the Santa Barbara Art Institute under veteran landscape painter Ray Strong. Larry continues to paint Western landscapes from his studio/home in Santa Barbara.*

Table of Contents

Before Newport Was Newport.................5

Envisioning a Commercial Harbor,
                    1864-1888.......13

Prosperous Years, 1889-1899.....................29

Newport for Sale, 1900-1914.....................41

Island Troubles, Floods, and New Jetty,
                    1915-1921......61

The Race against Silt, 1922-1928................69

Great Depression Brings Victories,
                    1929-1938.......87

World War II Brings Growth,
                    1939-1959.......97

Growth versus Charm, 1960-Present........103

Index 107

Sources 111

Acknowledgments...........................112

Corona del Mar to Huntington Beach, 1949

Building of Rock Groin West of Jetty

Before Newport Was Newport

For centuries, there was little to distinguish Newport from the lonely beaches and marshes stretching along much of California's coast. It was not until nature added a protective arm to a swamp to form Newport Bay that Southern California's world-renowned recreational harbor began to take shape. Despite this lucky accident, it would take visionary entrepreneurs and the dredging of millions of tons of silt before Newport could claim its title as the playground of the rich and famous.

During the Spanish era, Newport was largely ignored. While explorers were chronicling their journeys and claiming California for Spain, soldiers were building presidios (forts), and padres were establishing a powerful mission system, Newport was seen as little but a stretch of unwelcoming swamp. After **Juan Rodriguez Cabrillo** chronicled his 1542 exploration of the coast and claimed it all for the King of Spain, the Spaniards ignored California for more than two centuries. Only when England and Russia began to covet its rich land and convenient harbors did the King of Spain realize that he must assert ownership immediately by fortifying and settling the vast unexplored land. His first step to accomplish this was to send an overland expedition to identify sites for presidios and missions. Under the command of **Gaspar de Portola**, 67 men and 100 pack mules left San Diego in 1769 and proceeded north. Portola selected an inland route and missed Newport by 10 miles. Consequently, Newport was not selected for one of the presidios or missions.

Based on the findings of that expedition, Spain sent soldiers to build four presidios and padres to establish a string of missions along the coast. While, in theory, Spain placed its highest priority on its four presidios at Monterey, San Diego, San Francisco, and Santa Barbara, in practice, the presidios were ignored, poorly provisioned, and staffed with soldiers who were seldom paid. On the other hand, the missions, charged with converting the local tribes, were given authority over virtually all of the land. This land was to be used to teach the newly converted Native Americans ranching and agricultural skills in hopes that they would become "productive" Spanish citizens. In the process, mission land was cultivated, and many missions prospered.

Although the missions were given control of virtually all the land, there were some rare exceptions. One of these occurred in 1810 when **Jose Antonio Yorba** and **Juan Pablo Peralta** were awarded control of the 62,512 acres that encompassed today's cities of Santa Ana, Orange, Villa Park, Costa Mesa, and Tustin. Although aware that they retained this land only at the pleasure of the King of Spain, they named their large grant Rancho Santiago de Santa Ana and began running wild cattle on it. When it was divided and sold after the United States gained possession of California, its break-up provided land for settlers.

Throughout the Spanish era, from 1542 until 1821, explorers journeyed on without stopping, and soldiers were seldom seen traversing Newport's swampy marshland. Likewise, the padres from the two nearest missions, San Gabriel, established in 1771 and given jurisdiction of the Newport area, and San Juan Capistrano, established in 1776, almost never journeyed there but used Dana Point as their sea landing for supplies.

Local Tribes

For thousands of years, small tribal settlements flourished in the Newport area. The Spanish, who left detailed chronicles of other California tribes, seldom journeyed to Newport, and, as a result, did not record their observations of them. Nevertheless, plentiful artifacts found in the area have provided a great deal of information. Believed to have journeyed from the Great Basin area of Southern Oregon and Nevada, they were hunters and gatherers who used shells for beads and fishhooks and made arrowheads from obsidian. They also crafted decorative stone objects that were believed to have a religious significance. Their huts were dome-shaped and made of poles and brush.

Evidence confirms that they made canoes from bundles of tule caulked with the asphalt that washed up on the beaches. There is also strong evidence that they made planked canoes similar to those of the Catalina and Santa Barbara tribes. They used their canoes to venture far into the sea to fish and to trade, as evidenced by the abundance of implements made from Catalina soapstone that have been found in the Newport area.

Although the Spanish ignored Newport, the diseases they brought spread and, eventually, had a tragic impact on local tribes. Whether they sickened from the occasional soldier who journeyed into the area or caught diseases from the tribes that had frequent contact with soldiers and padres, before long, they experienced the deaths, lowered birth rates, and high infant mortality rates that plagued virtually all California tribes. Those who survived were either converted and went to one of the missions, or wandered farther inland to escape Spanish interference.

A River in Motion

Largely forgotten, the early decades of the 19th century might have been uneventful. However, during these years one of Newport's natural forces, the Santa Ana River, took a starring role in its transformation. Before recorded history, this river had meandered through the marshland to empty into the area today known as Back Bay. Later, it began to empty into Newport Bay, depositing silt to form the sandbars that became its islands. During flood times, this mighty river left its course through the bay. Instead, it cut a new course to the ocean by skirting the coastal mesa and emerging between Huntington Beach and Newport. Everywhere it went, the Santa Ana continued to deposit tons of silt, until it formed the barrier beach now known as Balboa Peninsula, the protective arm that encloses Newport Bay.

When the first United States team arrived in 1860 to survey the area, Balboa Peninsula already stretched south of the future site of the Pavilion. Although information about the extent of the peninsula in 1860 is invaluable, the survey was considered a failure. Using

7

a boat named the *Humboldt*, the survey team attempted to enter the bay by floating over the bar at the entrance. Their entry was hampered by "a frightful swell rolling and tumbling at all stages of the tide, making it dangerous to cross in boats of any kind." Unable to float over the bar, the *Humboldt* was soon caught by the swell. When it became clear that the boat was about to be wrecked and that the crew was in peril, the team left, promising to try again the following spring. With the outbreak of the Civil War, those plans were forgotten, and it was 15 years before the first hydrographic survey of Newport Bay was completed.

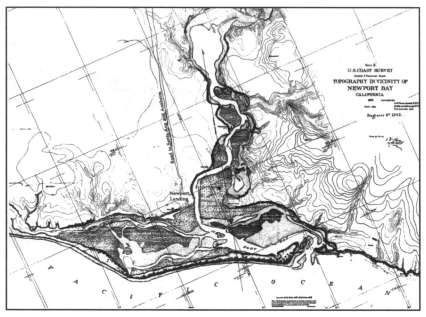

U.S.G.S. Survey of 1875

The Mexican Ranchos

When Mexico gained independence from Spain and took ownership of California in 1821, it was soon evident that the days of the missions were numbered. By 1833, Mexico passed the *Decree of Secularization* that took the land from the Catholic Church, and transferred virtually all of it to the Mexican government. Almost immediately, Mexican citizens rushed to petition for enormous land grants. Many of those who had proven their loyalty—or potential value—to the Mexican government were awarded huge expanses of land. Those awards ushered in the era of the Mexican rancho that is fondly known as "Old California."

Although the Yorba and Peralta families retained ownership of their rancho, large expanses of adjacent land were suddenly available and, by 1837, 35-year-old **Jose Sepulveda** was awarded land. Considered a difficult neighbor, he was immediately in conflict with the Yorbas and Peraltas, who complained that his herds wandered onto their property, accused him of stealing their cattle, and insisted that he was claiming even more land than he was granted.

Sepulveda's response was to ask for more land. After investigation of his request, the report to the Mexican governor concluded that Sepulveda "was a slippery and dishonest person who persistently and willfully sought to mislead lawful authorities" and that his request clearly contained incorrect information. Despite that damning testimony, by 1842, Sepulveda was granted a second tract of land. Combined, his land grants, named Rancho San Joaquin, included almost 47,000 acres and extended north to the Santa Ana Mountains, east to today's 55 Freeway, and south to Laguna Beach. Interestingly, it was later discovered that this grant did not include the land surrounding Newport Bay and the oceanfront at Newport Beach, for each was considered worthless.

Like most California ranchos, Sepulveda's Rancho San Joaquin was soon largely self-sufficient, producing most of its everyday needs by growing virtually all its produce and beef cattle. Sepulveda focused his attention on his grasslands and largely ignored the abundance of the ocean adjacent to his property. Comfortable on horseback, he probably never even ventured near the water, a fact noted by a bemused **Richard Henry Dana** in his wonderful recounting of this era in *Two Years Before the Mast*: "These people have no boats of their own. . . . It is difficult to fish from the back of a horse."

Everyday clothes were woven at the rancho, just as boots and saddles were crafted there. Luxury items, such as the lavish costumes and jewelry enjoyed by the Sepulvedas, were acquired through trade with visiting ships seeking hides and tallow, items in abundance at the rancho. Although some of that trade was conducted with Mexican ships, the only vessels legally allowed to trade in California waters under Mexican rule, much of this trade was conducted illegally with American and English ship captains. They were glad to smuggle luxury items to Sepulveda in exchange for his hides and tallow. This trade was so prevalent all along the coast that these hides became known as "California Dollar Bills."

Sepulveda's two land grants allowed him to live the life of a wealthy Mexican ranchero (rancher), a life symbolized by large families, lavish clothes, fine horses, and fiestas replete with gambling, rodeos, huge banquets, music, and dancing. He claimed to have 3000 horses and 14,000 cattle on his enormous rancho, and loved to host large family reunions to show off his 14 children. Like most Mexican rancheros, he was an avid gambler and enjoyed races, bear-roping contests, and bull and bear fights. Horse racing was one of his favorites, and legend has it that he won $25,000, 1000 horses, 500 heifers, and 500 sheep on one race.

Though quite comfortable during the Mexican era, life for Sepulveda and other rancheros got even better soon after America took possession of California. Whereas cattle had been valued only for their hides and tallow, the California Gold Rush of 1849 changed all of that. Suddenly, the wild, rangy Mexican cattle became the major food source of thousands of hungry prospectors craving meat. For a short period, the cattle were driven to the booming San Francisco area, and the rancheros basked in relative prosperity.

Demise of the Ranchos

As the excitement of the Gold Rush began to fade and the demand for wild cattle decreased, a series of events doomed the enormous ranchos. In 1852, six years after the United States took possession of California, a law requiring each ranchero to prove that he legally owned his land was passed. Rancheros had to survey their land and then submit maps, documents, and oral testimony to the Land

Commission. Although Sepulveda, like most rancheros, was able to prove legal ownership, his legal and survey fees were high. Added to that problem, the Americans introduced a new and shocking mandate to all rancheros who successfully proved ownership—taxes!

Whereas most rancho trading was barter, American lawyers and surveyors demanded cash. Although evidence exists that Sepulveda had acquired cash from gambling and selling beef during the Gold Rush—when he needed it most, his lavish lifestyle had caught up with him and he did not have ready cash. To pay his bills, he borrowed what he needed at usurious interest rates.

Just as the loans were coming due, a devastating three-year drought brought starvation to most of the cattle in California. When the rains returned, bills and taxes remained unpaid, cattle were dead, and a way of life was about to disappear forever. Sepulveda, plagued by his debts and the death of his herds, sold Rancho San Joaquin in 1864 to Flint, Bixby, Irvine, and Company for $18,000. The Yorbas and Peraltas fared no better, and their Rancho Santiago de Santa Ana was claimed by numerous heirs and eventually divided and sold by court order. In addition to the dissolution of the large ranchos, the land surrounding Newport Bay and the oceanfront at Newport Beach reverted to the State of California to be sold as swampland for $1 an acre. Many settlers journeying West after the Civil War came to California, and some came to Newport to buy the land that had suddenly become available.

Unlike many other areas in California, Newport was largely forgotten during the Spanish and Mexican eras. With the exception of the tragic demise of the local tribes, Spanish explorers, soldiers, and missionaries had minimal impact on the area. During Mexican rule, Newport's lonely beaches and swampy land held little attraction for the rancheros, and the area continued to be left largely untouched. It was the Santa Ana River, instead, that had the starring role. Its sweeping changes, combined with the break-up of the enormous ranchos set the stage for establishment of the Newport so many enjoy today.

Mudflat, Seen Beyond and to Left of Square-rigger, Became
Balboa Island

Envisioning a Commercial Harbor, 1864-1888

When Ranchos San Joaquin and Santa Ana were sold, some interesting entrepreneurs were drawn to the Newport area. Its abandoned beaches and primitive marshlands were about to disappear, as enormous changes loomed. Of those entrepreneurs, two pivotal men, **James Irvine** and **James McFadden**, emerged as leading visionaries, each with markedly different dreams for Newport. James Irvine arrived with a love of the land and plans to prosper by amassing a great deal of ranchland. James McFadden had an entirely different dream—he was going to create a town by dividing his land into small parcels and selling it to as many as would buy. Convinced that the more settlers he could entice to Newport, the sooner it would emerge as an important commercial center, he was Newport's first passionate promoter. While Irvine saw acres of ranchland rich with produce and herds, McFadden envisioned a bustling and prosperous town.

The Irvine Ranch

Since its inception, the Irvine Ranch has been intricately intertwined with the history of Newport. It was established when the debt-ridden Sepulveda was forced to sell his Rancho San Joaquin to Flint, Bixby, Irvine, and Company in 1864. **Benjamin Flint, Dr. Thomas Flint,** and **Llewellyn Bixby** were from Maine, while James Irvine was born in Ireland, the eighth of nine children of Anglo-Irish farmers. In 1846, at age 19, he joined the parade of immigrants crossing the Atlantic to New York. Years later, as the prosperous owner of an enormous ranch and the forefather of a foundation known for its philanthropic generosity, he recalled his trip: "I tell you a boy cast upon the world with not a dollar in his pocket. . . is in a position to appreciate the value of a helping hand."

13

During that trip he met **Collis Huntington**, soon to become one of the Big Four railroad magnates. Rather than cementing a friendship during that trip, the two visionary entrepreneurs had a disagreement that lasted throughout their lifetimes. When one of the Big Four's railroads, the Southern Pacific, needed to use Irvine's land to extend its rails from Santa Ana to San Diego, Irvine refused. Forced to give a railroad right-of-way through his land, he gave it to the Santa Fe, the Southern Pacific's competitor.

Irvine had spent two years in New York before journeying to San Francisco, via Panama, to participate in the Gold Rush of 1849. In addition to mining, he worked as a merchant, providing food for the ravenous miners. By 1854, he had been so successful that he was able to buy an interest in a San Francisco produce and grocery business. Though he prospered as a merchant, it was the land that attracted him, and, as soon as he had the money, he also began to invest in real estate.

Before long, he joined forces with the Flints and Bixby. When they had amassed enough money by providing meat to the hungry gold-seekers, they journeyed to Illinois to buy sheep. They drove approximately 2000 sheep to California, and, by the late 1850s, had established a wool business. Their timing could not have been better. As soon as they were established, the Civil War erupted. As the war made acquisition of cotton virtually impossible, wool was a welcome and profitable substitute. During the drought years of 1863 to 1865, their sheep, needing less forage, survived, while cattle were perishing by the thousands.

By the end of the drought, they had the cash to buy Sepulveda's Rancho San Joaquin. They were also ready to buy more land when the Yorbas' and Peraltas' Rancho Santiago de Santa Ana was dissolved by court order. Before long, they were the largest landholders in the region, owning over 100,000 acres. James Irvine took the lead in the company's ranch project and, by 1868, had built himself a home for the considerable sum of $1000 for his wife and one-year old son, **James II**. He focused his attention on ranching and tireless efforts to identify the most lucrative agricultural uses for his land. When he died in 1886, trustees, left in the control of the ranch until

James II turned 25, tried to sell it at auction. When this auction was declared illegal, his young son took over the reins of the huge ranch and accelerated efforts to increase its agricultural production.

James McFadden's Vision

In the 1860s, when the ranchos were being broken up and offered for sale, one early purchaser was James McFadden. One of 11 children of Scottish farmers who had settled in Delaware County, New York and a widower, McFadden first traveled to California in 1868. He visited Wilmington just before journeying to Newport and was immediately convinced that Newport Bay had far more potential than Wilmington as the region's premiere commercial deep-sea port —a conviction he maintained for almost four decades.

According to McFadden's memoirs, printed in the *Santa Ana Blade* of September 7, 1915:

> . . . the question of the depth of the water in the so-called San Joaquin slough [Newport Bay] became of interest, and through the assistance of a Mr. Goodrich, who was then the foreman of the San Joaquin Ranch, I secured the services of an old whaler who was herding a band of sheep for Mr. Goodrich, and who owned or secured a flat bottomed boat, and took me over the bar at what he claimed to be mean high tide. I found between 10 and 11 feet on the bar. This was disappointing to all of us, but it was claimed to be more than either Anaheim Landing or San Pedro had at the time.

Disappointed, but not discouraged, he and his brother, Robert, began purchasing land until they had acquired a large portion of the future site of Newport, including the oceanfront of Newport Beach, much of Balboa Peninsula, and the sandbars that were to become its islands.

The McFaddens' plan, quite different from Irvine's, was to sell as soon as possible. They subdivided their land and returned to their homes in the East to wait until enough land had been settled to support a town and, hopefully, the development of a seaport. They were optimistic that their land would sell quickly for the end of the Civil

War and the breakup of the ranchos had spurred migration to California. Intent on escaping the blood-soaked East and inspired by land offered at under $10 per acre, thousands arrived by steamer and wagon, seeking opportunity. According to the December 19, 1868 *Los Angeles Star:*

> *Not a day passes but long trains of emigrant wagons pass through town. . . . The great ranchos having been divided up, induces emigration, and we understand land is offered on such reasonable terms as to hold out superior inducements to settlers. For soil and climate, the southern counties are unequalled in the state. They have long been overlooked, and treated with but very little consideration, if not subject to contumely and contempt, but the time has at last arrived, when their waste places will become habitations and their deserts be made fruitful and blossom as the rose.*

This parade of settlers increased dramatically when the transcontinental railroad was completed in 1869. With the railroad, travel to California was suddenly infinitely easier. Although most of these settlers sought land away from coastal areas, some did gravitate to the area that was to become Newport, and, before long, the McFaddens sold some of their land.

Vaquero

In 1870, the first *Pacific Coast Pilot* was published, containing strong warnings about the danger of entering Newport Bay:

> *On the bar there is a very heavy swell in all stages of the tide, rendering it dangerous to cross in boats of any kind. . . . There is no safe anchorage off the entrance, and the low straight beach. . . affords no protection whatever. . . . The attempts to pass the bar were, in all cases, attended with risk, and the entrance may for general purposes, be regarded as impracticable.*

Despite the warning, homesteaders and settlers on farms as far inland as San Bernardino wondered about the potential of the unexplored bay. They sought convenient, inexpensive transportation for

16

their ever-increasing array of produce, and were not content to depend solely on the services offered by either the Port of Wilmington or Anaheim Landing (today's Seal Beach).

Captain Samuel Sumner Dunnels, a hotelkeeper in San Diego who dearly missed his seagoing days, was soon in a perfect position to explore its potential. He found a way to get on the water again by carrying passengers and delivering freight up and down San Diego harbor. The need for his services was so great that, by 1865, he had acquired and launched *Vaquero*, a 105-ton, sturdy, flat-bottomed wood-burning steamer designed for shallow-water river navigation. By 1870, Dunnels had expanded his route from San Diego harbor to include coastal ports north of the city.

As he traveled up and down the coast, he observed farmers' desperate need for an inexpensive and convenient transportation link. He also noted the intriguing, unexplored Newport Bay, then known as San Joaquin Bay, and wondered if it could provide the needed link.

Shallow-draft Sternwheeler Similar to *Vaquero*

Aware of the bar that blocked most ships from entering into its calm waters, Dunnels believed that he had the only boat that could successfully navigate it and was anxious to find out. In addition to seeking a prosperous new port that only he could use, Dunnels was probably seeking a way to avoid the most commonly used port in the area, Anaheim Landing, where he owed a great deal of money.

On September 10, 1870, the *Vaquero*, loaded with 5000 shingles and 5000 feet of lumber from San Diego, entered the bay slowly and cautiously. The entry was successful and uneventful. Dunnels unloaded near the convergence of the upper and lower bays and loaded *Vaquero* with local hay and grain. According to the September 15, 1870 *Los Angeles Star:*

> *The steamer Vaquero landed a cargo last Saturday at a point east of the Santa Ana River. . . . It is said that a good landing can easily be made at the place referred to. If this is a fact, it is of great importance to those settling on the fertile lands east of the Santa Ana River.*

Thrilled that he may have found a "new port," he soon built a small, temporary wharf there and scheduled regular trips. Also in 1870, Flint, Bixby, Irvine, and Company applied for a wharf franchise in the bay and, by November, it was granted. The location they had selected was adjacent to Dunnels' wharf, and they offered him use of their wharf. He declined. It was rumored that he refused because of a conflict with the ranch manager. He moved his wharf 200 feet down the beach and applied for a franchise of his own.

This franchise was granted, but Dunnels never used it due to financial woes. When the rush of settlers slowed in the early 1870s, businesses suffered. Dunnels had borrowed a great deal of money and could not withstand a decline in revenue. Additionally, *Vaquero* was more expensive to operate than he had anticipated as she was fueled by wood and burned a great deal on her ocean-going ventures. To compound his problems, Dunnels announced that he was opening up a new port for local farmers. He made a strategic mistake: Anaheim Landing and Wilmington were embroiled in an intense competition for dominance as Southern California's port. Neither port welcomed the news that a "new port" was about to compete for the agricultural trade. His Anaheim creditors moved quickly to make sure he was not successful in establishing the new port, by immediately pressing charges for unpaid debts. By April 1872, Dunnels had lost *Vaquero*, and commercial shipping ceased until the McFaddens were able to revive dreams of a commercial seaport.

Naming of Newport

During the early years, Newport had many names. It was sometimes known as Bolsa de Gengara (derived from an early tribal settlement, Geng-Na) and early maps referred to it as Bolsa de San Joaquin. When settlers from the East began to arrive, they wanted a new, easier to pronounce, and more prestigious name, and Newport was perfect. Although there is no proof concerning its origin, most believe that it came from one of two sources:

* Some credit Dunnels, who returned to San Diego after successfully crossing the bar in 1870, exuberantly proclaiming that he had found a "new port."

* Others believe that an Irvine Ranch employee sugested it during a meeting concerning commerce on the bay between the Irvines and the McFaddens.

Whatever the source, "Newport" was soon the widely accepted name for the remote and lonely tidal estuary dotted with sandbars that held such promise.

Transportation Needs Grow

James McFadden returned to Newport in 1873 to try farming the land that had not been sold. Although he planted corn as his staple crop, he also tried a variety of other crops. Although crops grew well, they were soon trampled by wandering cattle. Convinced that he needed to fence his property, he and his brother Robert went to San Francisco to purchase lumber for fencing. He had it shipped, but was surprised to discover that the need for lumber in Newport was so great that it was sold to other settlers (at a solid profit) before it had even arrived. When the same thing happened to a second shipment, the McFaddens knew they were out of farming and into the lumber business.

James McFadden journeyed East to prepare for his permanent move to Newport, while Robert and their brother, John, stayed to oversee lumber sales and sell land at prices ranging from $8 to $15 an acre. The influx of settlers had dwindled and land sales were slow, so slow that Robert even traded some of the land for hogs. Convinced that a convenient sea landing was essential if they were going to sell their land and succeed in their lumber business, they looked again at the marshy bay with the frightening sandbar blocking its entrance and began planning a landing there.

Concerned about the potential competition posed by the McFaddens, the owners of Anaheim Landing leased Dunnels' abandoned wharf and warehouse and employed two brothers named **Wilson**. Once Scandinavian fishermen, they rented boats and tackle, but were actually charged with using their base at the landing to stifle commercial activity in Newport Bay.

Their task became impossible when James McFadden arrived with his new wife and two daughters to settle in Newport, building a house that would be his home almost 40 years. Totally committed to the promise of Newport Bay, he immediately focused his energy on transforming Newport into the vibrant seaport he envisioned. To do this, he knew that he had get rid of the Wilson brothers and establish his own wharf and landing. He began by petitioning the state for the 20 acres of swampy beach on which portions of Dunnels' wharf and warehouse, occupied by the Wilson brothers, had been built.

By 1876, California agreed that it was swampland and sold it to him as tidelands for $1 an acre. McFadden then purchased the portions of Dunnels' wharf and warehouse that had not already been granted to him as tidelands and evicted the Wilson brothers. When they refused to leave, the McFadden brothers broke into the warehouse they now owned, took out all of the Wilsons' belongings and dumped them on a sail on the ground. A fight broke out when one of the Wilsons attacked with a crosscut saw. The good guys won when one Wilson was knocked out and the other tossed into the water. The Wilsons left the area and the McFaddens were free to focus their considerable energy on nurturing bay commerce at their Newport Landing.

The *Newport*

While working to acquire the land he needed for a landing, James McFadden also commissioned a vessel that could successfully navigate the sandbar. He ordered a 133.5-foot long, 25.5-foot wide steamer that only required 9 feet of water when fully loaded. Designed to have a large capacity, it could carry 1000 sheep, in addition to providing several staterooms for passengers. Weighing 331 tons, it was the first of a group of "steam schooners" that were unique to California. Capable of landing in small, rough coves up and down the coast, they were especially well-suited for carrying lumber from Northern California to the increasing number of settlers who had chosen California as their new home.

While his steam schooner was being built, McFadden improved a trail across the mesa to Santa Ana and brought supplies to Newport by wagon. He also encouraged schooners to venture into the bay to bring much-needed supplies and lumber. He was successful at enticing them through the shallow entrance, and, in the summer of 1875, six small schooners successfully entered the bay, bringing needed supplies. Despite their success, the schooner trade was both difficult and expensive. Requiring perfect weather and favorable silt conditions, it was dangerous even in the best of circumstances. Additionally, only the smallest of the schooners could even attempt to enter the bay, schooners so small that they could not carry enough cargo to net a profit large enough to justify the danger. Although the six schooners were successful at navigating the sandbar and swampy waters during the summer of 1875, all knew that schooner trade was not the convenient and economical option Newport needed, and anxiously awaited the completion of the McFaddens' new ship.

The McFaddens' steam schooner, *Newport*, was completed during the summer of 1875. When she arrived in Newport Bay on September 3, 1875, many believed that she would transform Newport into a commercial seaport. According to the September 11, 1875 *Anaheim Gazette:*

> *The McFaddens' new steamer arrived at Newport last Friday with a cargo of one hundred and fifty thousand feet of lumber. The arrival was quite an important event in the history of Southern Los Angeles County. The immense number of people in the farming section, of which Newport is the natural outlet, are, of course, deeply interested in having facilities for the shipment of their produce. On Sunday last . . . over 100 persons visited Newport for the purpose of inspecting the vessel and exchanging congratulations on the auspicious event.*

The *Newport* immediately began hauling cargo and was soon arriving every other week at high tide with lumber from Trinidad and transporting local meat, grain, produce, wool, and stock to San Francisco. In addition to meeting the needs of local small farmers, the *Newport* was welcomed by James Irvine, as it carried produce and stock for the increasingly prosperous Irvine Ranch. This powerful little steamer ushered in a 25-year era of McFadden domination of Orange County shipping.

Although the area was still sparsely settled and remote, the *Newport's* first years were good ones. An especially good year, 1876, brought new settlers and new customers for the *Newport*. Another cause for local exaltation was the demise of Anaheim Landing. When the Southern Pacific Railroad completed a spur from Anaheim to Los Angeles, Anaheim farmers no longer needed to transport their stock and produce by sea. They could use the faster and more efficient rails instead. It soon became clear that Anaheim Landing could not compete with the railroad, and it was abandoned. Although Newporters celebrated their victory over Anaheim Landing, the more astute may have seen the victory of rails over sea transport as the first of many that would virtually eliminate sea commerce.

Despite the progress during those good years, commerce in the bay was still a challenge. The average depth of the sandbar at high tide was only 8 feet, a foot less than the *Newport's* draft. The McFaddens had to time deliveries for extremely high tides to negotiate the bar. Adding to the difficulty was the discouraging fact that shifting sands constantly changed the entrance and channel, making navigation even more dangerous. On many occasions, Robert was tossed into the roiling water at the entrance to the bay while helping the *Newport* enter safely, and it soon became clear that something had to be done.

The McFaddens' solution was to build two lighters, barges that were propelled by poling. In addition to helping the *Newport* enter the bay, the lighters were used to transport cargo to the bay from ships anchored outside the entrance. Although an excellent solution to the challenge of low tides and shifting sands, even these lighters were not able to protect cargo when the breaking seas turned the entrance into a maelstrom. During those conditions, lumber was swept overboard, forcing the crew to retrieve as much as they could as it was swept onto the beach. That became such a common occurrence that the McFaddens established a lumberyard on the bluffs so that soaked wood could dry before being sold.

McFaddens' Difficult Years

The acquisition of the *Newport* ushered in several prosperous years for the young settlement—good years for the McFaddens. John took a leadership role in California politics, eventually becoming the Mayor of Santa Ana. James managed maritime business contracts and marketed McFadden enterprises, while remaining an impassioned promoter of Newport Bay. Robert supervised Newport Landing, working and living there until 1884.

Although 1876 was regarded as a good year with encouraging growth in business and the demise of its strongest competitor, Anaheim Landing, it also began a difficult era for the McFaddens. Despite the prosperity of that year, the drought of 1876-77 sowed the seeds of a depression. The ensuing decline of produce slowed growth, and trade at Newport stagnated.

It also saw the beginning of a four-year disagreement between Newport's founding fathers, McFadden and Irvine. Irvine had bought out his partners in 1876 and gained control of the enormous Irvine Ranch, later certified by the State Board of Equalization to cover 105,000 acres. The same year, when California granted McFadden the right to buy the 20 swampy acres of Newport Bay at $1 each, Irvine claimed that McFadden had been acting as his agent when the request was submitted and that the 20 acres belonged to him. Irvine demanded his land and threatened to evict the McFaddens from the contested land, including their wharf and warehouse. Newporters watched the conflict with concern, for they knew that if the McFaddens were evicted from their landing, the promising commercial activities of the *Newport* would be severely crippled, if not destroyed.

The conflict lasted until 1880, when a judge declared that the land belonged to James Irvine and that he had the right to evict the McFaddens. Popular opinion did not support the decision. Not only were the McFaddens popular civic promoters, they also provided extremely important shipping services to the young community. Many worried that Newport would wither without the McFaddens. Unlike the McFaddens, Irvine did not enjoy local support. Citizens blamed him for the fact that they did not have a railroad. They knew that his refusal to give the Southern Pacific a right-of-way across his ranch was delaying the completion of a transportation link to San Diego. Irvine was sensitive to public opinion and allowed the McFaddens to continue landing on the beach and to lease some of the contested land. Pleased with the compromise, the McFaddens continued to base their shipping business there and even expanded their warehouse to three stories.

Still, troubles for the McFaddens continued. The sandbar, always challenging, was getting even more difficult to cross. As farmers began tilling the soil, they cleared the willows and brush that had been trapping much of the silt. Without the brush, the bay and

24

entrance silted up rapidly. The channel soon became so difficult to navigate that the McFaddens had to hire a pilot to help the *Newport* navigate its ponderous journey to their landing. As silting worsened, the channel shifted so often that the pilot was soon forced to sound it before each arrival. Despite his soundings, the Newport frequently went aground and cables had to be installed along the route to pull her out of the mud.

In April 1878, the *Newport* was stuck on the bar again amid ferocious waves, endangering both boat and crew. Lifeboats were lowered for the mate and three sailors. When the mate disobeyed orders and rowed directly into the surf, the lifeboat capsized. Watching in horror, the captain lowered another boat for himself and two more crew and began rowing to the rescue. Their lifeboat also capsized in the unrelenting waves, and all seven men floundered helplessly in the breaking waves. While two crewmen were saved, five drowned, including the *Newport's* captain. The McFaddens mourned the loss, and many believe that James never fully recovered from his grief.

Those years also brought what James McFadden considered to be a betrayal. Strongly supportive of eventually getting railroad service to his beloved Newport, he contributed thousands of dollars to the Southern Pacific so that it would extend rails to Santa Ana. As soon as the railroad to Santa Ana was completed in 1877, the Southern Pacific mounted a war against the McFaddens' shipping business by offering cheaper rates to local farmers. For just over a year, the McFaddens continued to operate the *Newport* at a loss of more than $6000. Finally, in November 1878, they gave up and sold their steamer to the Pacific Coast Steamship Company. Although she continued to journey between San Francisco and Newport Landing each week, her trips north to collect lumber were over forever, and settlers were again forced to depend on schooners for their lumber. Unable to enter the bay, the schooners anchored offshore while lumber was either floated ashore or poled to the landing on one of the McFaddens' barges. Although Robert McFadden continued to operate the landing and act as the steamship company's agent, James McFadden's visionary passion for the commercial potential of the bay no longer fueled the gutsy steam schooner named *Newport*.

Big Changes for Newport Beach

By the early 1880s, the Santa Fe Railroad began to serve Orange County, breaking the strangling monopoly of the Southern Pacific. Finally, the produce from Orange County's rich agricultural land began to bring a profit to farmers. Reflecting optimism and pride, the *Los Angeles Times* reported on August 3, 1883:

A Few Things That Newport Can Crow Over

* *That we have raised the most corn to the acre than any other locality in the county.*
* *That we have raised the largest beet that was ever raised in the county, weight 230 pounds.*
* *That we raise and export more fat hogs than any one shipping point in the valley.*
* *That we have the best resort for pleasure seekers in the county.*
* *That we have the advantage over any other place for shipping our produce, either from Newport harbor or the Santa Ana depot.*
* *That we will soon have a No. 1 pork-packing house; also a large cheese factory is in progress.*

The boom brought growing demands for lumber. For a while, the McFaddens tried to meet the need with the schooners anchored offshore, but it soon became clear that a new solution was needed. In 1887, after years of agitation, the federal government finally approved an appropriation for a survey to determine the feasibility of dredging and building jetties at the entrance of the bay.

Unfortunately, the difficult entrance again dashed hopes for a commercial port in Newport Bay. Army Corps of Engineers surveyors were forced by fog to spend the night in a rowboat outside the entrance before entering the bay. They were not happy. Several weeks later, their discouraging report was released that estimated a cost of over $1.5 million to construct two jetties and dredge the bay. According to the 1888 report by the Chief of Engineers, **W. H. H. Benyaurd**:

> It [Newport] was at one time the shipping and distributing point for the adjacent county. The construction of the railroad to Santa Ana, 12 miles distant, changed the method of transportation and the business of the harbor declined. One small steamer arrives twice a month from San Francisco. This, with an occasional small lumber vessel, constitutes the carrying trade of the harbor. The cost of construction and maintenance of the works intended to give a permanent increase of depth at the harbor is entirely incommensurate with the advantages that would accrue to commerce.

Based on his report of a minimal amount of trade, Newport Bay expenditures were denied, while large appropriations for the more promising ports at San Pedro and Wilmington were approved.

Despite extreme disappointment with the findings, the report did offer a suggestion that resulted in great changes to Newport. The engineers noted the quiet water off the beach west of the entrance. They recommended a hydrographic survey of the area, for they suspected that the quiet water signified unusually deep water—the perfect location for a large commercial wharf. They were right, and Newport was soon swept into its glorious decade as a flourishing shipping center.

In a few short decades, Newporters welcomed settlers, watched Irvine Ranch prosper, cheered the **Vaquero** and the **Newport** as they struggled through the treacherous entrance to the bay, and saw their hopes for shipping in the bay wither. Instead, by 1888, this young settlement began to turn its attention from its swampy and fickle bay to the promise of a large commercial wharf on their beach. And they watched with hope as it neared completion.

Ladies Walking in Newport, 1906

Parking Lot, 1910

28

Prosperous Years, 1889-1899

Turning from disappointment at the Army Corps of Engineers' refusal to support bay improvements to the promise of a beach-based seaport, the McFaddens moved quickly to build a large commercial pier. By focusing their energy and resources, they completed the wharf by late 1888. Instead of fruitlessly fighting their sandbar, Newporters were finally able to capitalize on their geography by building a wharf in the deep calm water where Newport Beach's Municipal Pier stands today. Extending 1300 feet into the ocean, towering 19 feet above the high water mark, and spanning a width of 60 feet, the wharf was designed to transform Newport into a commercial seaport. And, for a decade, that is exactly what it accomplished. On January 9, 1889, Newport Beach's first ship, *Eureka*, arrived with 10 tons of cargo and Newport's short-lived commercial prosperity was born. According to legend, as the *Eureka* let out a long whistle blast to celebrate its arrival, the wife of the wharfinger gave birth to a son.

The wharf was a success, and suddenly Newport was a port in deed as well as in name. In addition to the tons of cargo that arrived daily,

Photo Courtesy of Newport Beach Historical Society

McFaddens' Wharf in 1892

local farmers were jubilant about the convenient, inexpensive transportation link it provided. Virtually all products from small farms, especially grain, meat, eggs, and citrus fruit, were now conveniently and inexpensively shipped from the wharf. It also served the needs of the area's largest landowner, the Irvines. Although James Irvine had died, his son, **James Irvine II,** was beginning to experiment with large-scale farming, in addition to ranching. The wharf fit his needs perfectly, and he used it to ship everything, specifically barley, beans, and sugar beets, to market.

Ships came from Washington, Oregon, and ports all over California, and, although most were steamers, large schooners were also seen at the wharf during those years. Before long, Newport was on the regular delivery route for over 70 ships. During its busiest years, three ships were being unloaded while others anchored nearby waiting their turn. The completion of the pier spurred the development of a small settlement of tents and rough wooden buildings at its base to house port-related businesses. It also became known as the best fishing pier along the coast due to its close-in deep water, and began to attract both professional and amateur fishermen.

Railroad Spur to Wharf

The year the wharf was completed also saw the birth of Orange County and the arrival of Newport's first tourists. The McFaddens led a drive to separate from Los Angeles County. After consistent agitation led by James McFadden, the area successfully gained its independence from Los Angeles County, and, in March 1889, Orange County was born. In addition to bringing Newport Pier's first ship and independence from Los Angeles County, 1889 also brought the first tourists as the road to Santa Ana was improved and a bridge over the west end of the bay was built to connect the peninsula to the mainland.

Newport's Railroad

James McFadden knew that an inexpensive and convenient way to transport goods from the wharf to the railroad in Santa Ana was essential for Newport to realize its promise as a commercial center. With hopes of completing a railroad at the same time as the wharf, McFadden began building the Santa Ana and Newport Railroad. According to legend, he measured the distance between Newport and Santa Ana by driving the route by wagon with a rag tied to his wheel. By counting the number of revolutions, he was able to calculate the number of rails and ties he needed.

Once he knew what was needed, he simply had to find a way to get everything to Newport. He first ordered four small (16-foot) flatcars that were brought by boat from San Diego. Next he ordered the ties and rails. They were brought by boat and then transported to the railhead using the flatcars drawn by horses. Despite his good planning and creative solutions, delays made it impossible to complete the railroad as planned. It took until February 1891, two years after the opening of the wharf, for McFadden's railroad to carry its first cargo.

The station was located at the wharf, and rails were built on the pier. At its busiest, the railroad employed 100, making it Orange County's largest employer. Before long, services and shops needed by these employees were built near the pier, and included a boarding house, water tank, candy and curio stores, and a feedlot. (When horses and mules were banned from the beach, this feedlot became Newport's first parking lot.) Early each morning, fishermen provided food for the settlement by rowing their dories over the surf to catch the abundant stocks of fish that were sold by their wives near the base of the wharf.

In 1892, a severe storm from the southeast destroyed 600 feet of the pier. When the pilings were replaced, they penetrated the ocean floor a full 15 feet, rather than the original eight feet, and there was confidence that the wharf could successfully withstand the winterstorms. During the '92 storm, three railroad flatcars were dumped into the ocean. Within a few weeks, two of these cars drifted to shore. The third seemed to have disappeared until 1915, when it was seen floating just offshore. When it was dragged to shore, it was in such good condition that it was exhibited throughout the nation as an example of superlative American manufacturing.

Photo Courtesy of Newport Beach Historical Society

Village near the Base of the Wharf

1890s Daytrippers Pouring out of Rail Cars at Wharf

And People Came

Although designed to be a transportation link for freight, in August 1891, the railroad brought its first excursion train with over 200 passengers to Newport. According to reports, passengers were charged 25 cents each so that the agent could buy himself a chair. When the vacationers arrived, the *Los Angeles Times* of August 16, 1891 reported that they found a very appealing place to play:

> *Newport is very lively just now. There are probably from 75 to 100 tents pitched on the sand between Newport Bay and the ocean, besides several small rough frame buildings. A pavilion has been erected where people may recline in the shade while watching the bathers. The water was clear and remarkably clear of seaweed. Of the 500 people who enjoyed themselves at the beach, at least two-thirds enjoyed a dip and a swim. At least 100 buggies, wagons and other vehicles were counted near the feed stables. For some reason not fully explained, no trains are to be run on Sunday.*

Always entrepreneurial, McFadden responded to the influx of summer and weekend visitors by acquiring ownership of half of the peninsula in 1892 when he convinced the government that it was swampland and, under the Tidelands Act, cost $1 an acre. He immediately platted the area and leased lots for $12 to $18 a year to those who wanted to build cottages. By the mid-1890s, although still deserted during the winter, there were a few simple summer cottages dotting the area. Though most built on the beach, some selected the bay near the site of today's Balboa Pavilion. Those who chose the bay rather than the oceanfront acquired small sailboats so that they could cavort in its fickle winds. Before long, seven families owned boats and began to challenge one another, thus beginning Newport's long-standing tradition of sailboat racing.

As more and more cottages began to appear along the coast, a few began to suspect that Newport could become California's playground, the perfect escape from the congestion of the city. McFadden acted on that vision by building the Newport Hotel near the pier. He lured guests by offering free rail tickets. As his hotel was the only place, other than a makeshift campsite, for visitors to stay, it prospered.

Sunday Afternoon near the Wharf

Many believe that it also prospered because rail passengers who came to the beach to play on Saturday were forced to stay until Monday. Strictly religious, the McFaddens refused to let their railroad operate on Sunday. While the more affluent simply spent the weekend at the Newport Hotel and returned home or to work on Monday after enjoying their weekend, the lack of Sunday service was inconvenient for most workers. If they wanted to come to play on the beach on Sunday, their only day off, they could not use the McFaddens' railroad and were forced to travel by wagon or horseback.

Railroads

Railroads played a central role in the stories of many California towns, and Newport was no exception. Hoping to ease their transportation challenges, farmers—the economic foundation of California—were desperate to get the railroad to their town and were willing to pay to entice it there. The Big Four, **Leland Stanford,** Collis P. Huntington, **Charles Crocker**, and **Mark Hopkins,** were acutely aware of this desperation and became wealthy profiting from it. The Big Four partnered in 1861 to establish the Central Pacific, charged with completing the nation's first transcontinental railroad by building rails east from San Francisco to Ogden, Utah to connect with the westbound Union Pacific Railroad.

By 1862, Congress had enacted the Pacific Railroad Bill that gave the Central Pacific a 400-foot right of way along its entire route, authorized substantial loans, and sweetened the deal by giving its owners 128,000 acres for every 100 miles of rail they completed. The Big Four pushed to build their railroad quickly. Not only would they get more land for each 100 miles completed, but also the price of the land they were given would skyrocket as soon as rail service reached it. Unfortunately, despite their efforts to move quickly, progress was slow. With debts mounting, the Big Four went to Congress again and, in 1864, were rewarded when Congress doubled the land grants (256,000 acres for every 100 miles!) and authorized other financial incentives to keep the rails moving East.

By 1865, several years before the completion of the transcontinental railroad, the Big Four established another railroad, the Southern Pacific, specifically designed to expand their empire in California, pay off their transcontinental railroad debts, and protect their personal fortunes. They offered a convenient transportation link to farmers and towns. In exchange, they demanded—and got—enormous amounts of money and free land all along their route. Once their rails had been built, they used their transportation monopoly to force customers to pay high, and ever-increasing, rates. When a farmer complained that these rates were putting him out of business, a Southern Pacific auditor would review his books to determine the highest rate he could pay and not go bankrupt.

The route between Orange County and San Diego was essential for the Big Four to maintain its monopoly. They faced a powerful enemy. James Irvine refused to let the Southern Pacific proceed south over his land, partially due to his disagreement with Collis Huntington on the ship many years before. The Santa Fe Railroad was challenging the Southern Pacific's monopoly and sued Irvine for access. The race to San Diego heated up when, one weekend, Southern Pacific crews began laying rails on the Irvine Ranch without permission. When ranch hands with shotguns confronted the crews, work stopped. Convinced that he would be forced to give access to one of the railroads, Irvine finally gave the Santa Fe permission to build its rails on the Irvine Ranch.

Ever seeking to maintain their monopoly in the face of competition, the Big Four expended a great deal of effort and money to expand their web of rails and to buy out all competitors. They were successful, and, by the mid-1880s, the Southern Pacific had achieved domination of California's transportation by controlling 85% of its rails and shipping companies. Buying out competitors was often easy, as many sold as soon as the right price was offered. For those who would not sell, the Big Four had a strategy. They established a dummy company that appeared to be competing with the Southern Pacific. Then, that company, silently owned by the Southern Pacific, purchased the line the Big Four wanted to control. This ploy worked repeatedly throughout California and was about to happen in Newport.

By 1898, the McFaddens' Santa Ana and Newport Railroad was in need of new equipment and extensive overhaul of the roadbed and rails. When **Colonel W.H. Holabird** approached James and Robert with an offer to buy their railroad and pier for $400,000, they were interested. The colonel said that he was the agent for **J. Ross Clark**, a millionaire U. S. Senator, who owned a sugar beet factory in Los Alamitos. According to the colonel, Clark was angry that the Southern Pacific was charging him so much and wanted to buy the McFaddens' railroad and extend it to his factory to circumvent the high Southern Pacific rates.

Photo Courtesy of Newport Beach Historical Society

Terminus of the Santa Ana and Newport RR

Still feeling bitter and betrayed by the Southern Pacific for its rate war that had forced them to sell the *Newport*, they were intrigued by Clark's plan to circumvent the Southern Pacific and seriously considered the offer. After discussing it with officials of the Santa Fe Railroad, the McFaddens decided to accept the offer and the railroad and pier were sold in January 1899. For a while, rumors flew as locals tried to determine why a millionaire of Clark's stature was interested in Newport. According to an April 9, 1899 *Los Angeles Times* article:

37

J. Ross Clark, the millionaire sugar-beet man and United States Senator from Montana, is reaching out in his investments in this section of Southern California. Only about a month ago he purchased the Santa Ana and Newport Railroad, extending from Santa Ana to Newport Beach, and thence to the famous peat lands, located a few miles south of the town of Westminster.

Newport Beach is becoming quite a popular resort, the property of the company being considered worth about $50,000 or $60,000.

By May, Clark began rail service on Sundays, to the delight of many. Its first Sunday trip was eagerly reported in the Monday, May 8, 1899 *Los Angeles Times:*

Sunday railroad service between Santa Ana and Newport Beach was inaugurated today (May 7). A stiff coast wind was blowing in the morning, with the promise of an unpleasant day at the beach. The public, however, showed its appreciation of the service by turning out in large numbers to patronize the road.

The railroad between Santa Ana and Newport Beach has been in operation for more than five years, but not until the road passed into the hands of the Clarks were arrangements made to run Sunday trains. This new feature is meeting with popular approval, and as the summer season approaches, the capacity of the road will no doubt be taxed to furnish suitable rolling stock to accommodate the public.

Popular approval was short-lived. Less that a month later, shock waves hit Newport when it was discovered that Clark had relinquished ownership of the railroad to the enemy, the Southern Pacific. Although never proven, it is highly likely that Clark was acting as an agent for the Southern Pacific throughout the negotiations.

Although vacationers loved rail service to Newport on Sunday, many farmers were loyal to the McFaddens and refused to use the Southern Pacific. James Irvine used the Santa Fe Railroad and sent

38

his products all the way to San Diego to avoid using the Southern Pacific. Some did use the Southern Pacific and were shocked to watch rates rapidly increase until it cost as much to transport goods to Newport Wharf as to San Pedro, a far longer distance. It was not long before the high rates killed commerce at Newport, and the wharf's last commercial shipment arrived in January 1907. The rails were removed from the wharf and the outer 144 feet were torn down, reputedly because they had become unsafe. Overnight, Newport's era as a vibrant shipping port had ended, and its decade of commercial prosperity was over.

Bay Hopes Continue

Even at the height of shipping from the wharf, James McFadden never lost his conviction that the bay would be a perfect commercial port and backed up this conviction by continuing to agitate for the federal funding needed to build jetties and to dredge. He was not alone in his pleas to Washington. The federal government was being barraged by requests for the funding needed to improve a number of California's harbors. Although Newporters staunchly maintained that the funding should be given to them, the real contenders for funding were Santa Monica and San Pedro.

The Southern Pacific marshaled its political capital to convince the government to fund improvements at Santa Monica, for they controlled that port. Opponents fought fiercely against this and supported allocations to San Pedro, a publicly-owned, deep-water port. Finally, in 1899, after six years of study and deliberation, it was announced that the Southern Pacific had lost, and that $3 million had been allocated to improve the port at San Pedro. Although good news for California, the enormous allocation not only totally ignored the bay's potential for commercial prominence, but also gave the final, killing blow to Newport's wharf. The enormous federal allocation would so significantly improve San Pedro that Newport would have no chance of competing successfully.

In many ways, 1899 was a devastating year for the McFaddens. Not only had the bay lost its bid for federal funding, but the railroad had also been finessed away, and the wharf was quickly dying. James was disappointed with the government's decision, disgusted with the Southern Pacific, and still mourning the drowning deaths of the *Newport's* crew. Disheartened and saddened, convinced that he had failed and that his dreams for Newport would never be realized, he made plans to leave. By 1902, he had sold all of his holdings: the Newport town site (including the Newport Hotel), one-half of Balboa Peninsula, and the swamplands that were to become Harbor, Lido, and Balboa Islands, totaling approximately 900 acres. He sold his property for an undisclosed amount, suspected to be $35,000, with $5000 down, to **William S. Collins** and **A. C. Hanson**, who immediately began offering lots for sale at prices ranging from $150 for inside lots, to $300 for oceanfront property.

Although James McFadden left, he remains a central figure in Newport's story. His dreams for the desolate, swampy land, as well as his considerable energy, political savvy, and business acumen, left an important legacy. With his departure came Newport's next generation of promoters: the developers with their dredges. Newport's decade as a commercial port was over, as were its days as a rough supply center and remote holiday spot for campers. Instead, it was about to enter the 20th century, replete with "For Sale" signs, dredges, fast-talking agents, and vacationers seeking sun and stunning beaches. Although it would take half a century to actualize, Newport's transformation into a world-class destination was about to begin.

Newport for Sale, 1900-1914

By the beginning of the 20th century, significant changes began to impact Southern California. Only a few decades earlier, ranching and agriculture had dominated the economy and controlled most of the land. During those years, its cities were little but service and supply centers. By 1900, cities had begun to mushroom, engulfing ever-increasing expanses of land. Suddenly, many Southern Californians were city-dwellers. As a sign of the growing dominance of cities in Southern California, Los Angeles had 102,000 residents by 1900 and had not even entered its era of tremendous growth. Although Orange County was still sparsely populated, with a total population of only 5000, Santa Ana, its largest city, was also entering an era of growth.

Not tied to their jobs day and night as were ranchers and farmers, working class city-dwellers began to experience a relatively new concept—leisure time. Although most worked six days a week, growing numbers found some time for recreation. Uninterested in spending their free time at home in their congested cities, many escaped whenever possible to nearby beaches. Although the beaches closer to Los Angeles, such as Redondo and Santa Monica, felt their impact immediately, it was not long before Newport's beaches were crowded on sunny weekends, full of escapees from cities as far-flung as Pasadena and Riverside.

In 1902, Newport began to capitalize on the lure of its beaches and its budding tourist trade by hosting a grand Fourth of July celebration. A stunning success, it was glowingly described by the *Los Angeles Times:*

Newport Beach Never So Overrun Before

At least 8000 people visited Newport Beach today, which is the largest crowd this seaside town has even seen. Almost everyone from Santa Ana headed for the beach, and there were a good many people from other Southern California towns as well. The crowd enjoyed a patriotic day. The town was well decorated, and there was even a free clambake.

Hundreds of tourists took trains from Riverside and Los Angeles to Santa Ana, the jumping off point to catch the rail line to Newport. Two thousand people waited at Santa Ana for the train to the beach. Only a small number could be squeezed into the coaches, and other cars had to be added to the line. The bathhouses were so overrun that they weren't able to handle the crowd that wanted to change their clothing to swim.

Patriotic speeches were given in the afternoon. They were followed by a display of water sports at the end of the wharf. The program ended with a realistic naval battle and the blowing up of a miniature battleship. Tonight there will be a splendid fireworks display ending with a very credible representation of the eruption of Mount Pelee.

Red Car

As the popularity of excursions to the beach grew, **Henry Huntington,** nephew of Collis Huntington of the Southern Pacific's Big Four, hatched a plan to capitalize on a growing fascination with the ocean. He purchased the Los Angeles electric railway system and, by 1901, had filed for incorporation as the Pacific Electric Railway Company. He immediately expanded the rail line so that it linked Los Angeles to Southern California's coastal towns by providing a fast, clean, inexpensive way to get to the beach. He was successful and, suddenly, beach excursions became easy, affordable, and fun.

Known as "Red Cars," the electric railway system progressed quickly south toward Newport. By 1902, it had reached Bay City (originally Anaheim Landing, and renamed Seal Beach in 1915), and had stretched to Huntington Beach by 1904. Everywhere the Red Cars stopped, they brought thousands of visitors and triggered surging land values. Soon, beach towns began to vie for their own Red Car stations. Newport was no exception and, eventually, was successful in enticing the Red Cars south to its sparsely-used beaches and still-swampy bay. Their arrival introduced an enormous number of visitors to Newport and began its transformation into a recreational destination.

Newport's First Developer

The McFaddens' sale of their Newport land to Collins and Hanson was the first of many 20th century newsworthy land deals. On May 24, 1902, the *San Francisco Call* reported:

Newport Beach Passes into Syndicate Hands
One of the most important real estate deals in the history of Orange County was consummated today when Newport Beach, the foremost seaside resort of this section, passes from the hands of the Newport Wharf and Lumber Company to a syndicate of L.A., S.F., N.Y., and Riverside capitalists, who will take immediate possession of the property and expend large sums in its further development. The transfer includes the hotel, warehouses, cottages and all holdings of the Newport Wharf and Lumber Company at the beach, covering the 880 acres of the resort.

Although most of the land that Collins and Hanson purchased was undeveloped, a portion was already occupied—the McFaddens had leased land to vacationers who built beach cottages. They had also let fishermen and wharf workers construct rough dwellings near the wharf. Collins and Hanson, anxious to market Newport as a luxurious resort, knew that they must rid the area of leasees and squatters. They notified all leasees that they must buy the land for $125 by June 1, a mere eight days later, or forfeit their cottages. While some purchased their lots and others simply left, the number who had to be evicted was relatively small. They also tried to get the fishermen and wharf workers who were squatting on their property to leave, but, to their credit, they let most of them stay.

As soon as that pesky problem had been addressed, Hanson and Collins began selling Newport as a luxurious recreational community. Although much of Newport was swampy and unappealing, they began their marketing efforts by naming Newport "Queen of the Beaches." Their campaign began to pay off when West Newport, the area west of the wharf, was sold to the Orange County Improvement Association for $80,000. The president of the association, **Stephen Townsend**, had a successful track record in developing and selling land, and led West Newport's development by dredging it, dividing it into subdivisions, creating bathing pools and canals, and offering it for sale. Soon, a group of buyers came by boat from Long Beach and bought a large amount of land. That success spurred a real estate boom there, and, before long, there were 48 agents selling land and six clerks writing West Newport sales contracts. Options were sold and resold and lot prices soared from $400 to over $1800. At the height of this land boom, prices at Redondo Beach plummeted and deflation swept the coast. Almost immediately, the real estate agents left West Newport and sought the next booming development.

These agents found what they were seeking when Collins announced that the Red Cars would soon be arriving in Newport. By that time, Hanson had dropped out of the partnership and had left Collins to develop Newport on his own. Young, handsome, fast-talking, and entrepreneurial, Collins soon found another partner who had the money and power to make Collins' dreams for

Newport come true—Henry Huntington. Excited with the knowledge of what Huntington's Red Cars would do for land sales, he gave Huntington a 100-foot right of way along the peninsula, plus the land between present 9th and 19th streets, and the mudflat that would soon become Lido Island in exchange for $37,500 and Huntington's promise to bring his wondrous Red Cars to Newport.

Red Cars

When it was announced that the Red Cars would be arriving, lots began to sell. Prices leapt from $125 to $250 for ordinary lots and soared even higher for the prize lots. Soon, a number of lots had been sold and a few cottages built. Those who had purchased underwater lots clung to the hope that the promised dredging would turn their swampy lot into prime real estate. All enthusiastically awaited the arrival of the Red Cars and the visitors they would bring.

When the first Red Car arrived in Newport the summer of 1905, it was pulling 80 passenger cars full of enthusiastic vacationers. Its celebratory arrival, colored by some disappointing observations, was described by the *Daily Telegram:*

> *It was a great day for Newport. As early as 10 a.m., Ocean Front Avenue was crowded with a surging mass of people. The completion of the new extension of the electric road will, it is believed, result in a great boom for "Newport by the Sea." It is hoped, however, that future visitors won't experience the problems that surfaced today. It took three hours to cover 22 miles from Long Beach to Newport. The reason for the delay was that there is only a single track south of Huntington Beach.*

> *There was no excuse, however, for the price gouging that resulted. The advertised rate from Long Beach was 40 cents round trip. Those who neglected to buy the tickets at the Long Beach station, or who boarded cars any place down the line, were charged 75 cents.*

> *It certainly seems that the arrival of the electric car line has triggered a massive real estate boom in the old town.*

Every other man one meets is a real estate dealer or agent, and all appear to be getting rich.

When it was announced that the Red Cars would arrive at the Balboa Pavilion on July 4, 1906, the town got busy. A hotel was built on the present site of the Balboa Post Office in a mere 10 days! When they arrived, another celebration was staged to welcome the visitors they brought.

Balboa Hotel

Newport was now connected to the mass transit system. The ride from Los Angeles took just over an hour, and, when working as planned, Red Cars arrived each hour, introducing thousands to the best fishing grounds in the Southland, in addition to extraordinary beaches. Arriving passengers were greeted with a free lunch hosted by promoters with lots to sell. Promising passengers were then treated to free boat excursions to inspect lots. The task of the promoters was challenging, as much of the land they were offering for sale was still underwater. Although prosperity came slowly to Newport, and towns nearer Los Angeles, like Redondo Beach, were favored at first, Newport did become a popular destination. Red Car excursions offered thousands of city-dwellers their first view of

Newport, many of whom fell in love with its picturesque bay and stunning ocean sunsets.

Balboa Peninsula

Edward Abbott collected shells for a hobby and found a treasure trove at Balboa Peninsula. He soon fell in love with the area, and, in 1892, purchased a portion of the peninsula from the state as swamp/overflow land for $1 an acre under the Tidelands Act. When he built his home there, he became Balboa Peninsula's first resident. He also became Newport's first commuter, for he drove to Santa Ana to work each day. In addition to his home, he built a small pier near today's ferry crossing that became known as Abbott's Landing.

Painfully aware that his low-lying land could be flooded and even swept away at any time, Abbott knew that he had to secure his vulnerable property. He decided that the best erosion control would be a concerted effort to plant a large number of trees on the peninsula, and he began the planting. Unfortunately, the soil was too sandy and the trees died—until he began putting a shark in each tree hole to enrich the soil. With this added nutrient, the trees thrived, and

Photo Courtesy of Newport Beach Historical Society

Balboa's Pavilion

47

the peninsula stabilized. As the peninsula became less vulnerable, more and more came to play. Many brought their sailing skiffs, and the days of bay races began.

By 1905, the Balboa Pavilion was built. As there was still no road on the peninsula, construction materials had to be barged in. Once the Pavilion was completed, challenges continued, for few came. It was simply too difficult to get there, for visitors had either to brave crossing the unpredictable bay on a small skiff, or trek down the roadless peninsula. Only when the Red Car line was completed the following year did the Pavilion begin to prosper as the recreational center of the region.

Once the Red Cars started arriving daily, land sales on the peninsula increased and summer homes began to appear. **Everett Chance** bought eight old tent houses for $85 and moved them to a location adjacent to the Pavilion. Vacationers loved them, and they were rented every weekend during the summers. Eventually, a surfaced road along the peninsula was completed and the area was renamed "Balboa" by **E. J. Louis**, the vice-consul for Peru, based in Los Angeles.

Peninsula businesses established to serve residents and vacationers prospered. Rather than journeying to Newport for supplies and services, the peninsula soon became self-sufficient, offering all the goods and services one might need, including two grocery stores, a tackle store, three restaurants, a candy store, a pharmacy, a plumber, two electricians, a dry goods store, a hardware store, a drycleaners, a watchmaker, several garages for the new "horseless carriages," a battery repair station, several furniture stores, a cobbler, several barber shops, two churches, a fire department, and a bank. Some manufacturing enterprises were even established, including two boatbuilders and the machine shop Collins used to build the dredge that would shape Balboa Island. In addition to this commercial self-sufficiency, Balboa residents established their own Chamber of Commerce, and the town quickly developed its own character, replete with unique political issues and opinions, often at odds with those of Newport.

Vacationers were also well-served, for the peninsula boasted a wide assortment of recreational activities, including fishing and sailing expeditions, two poolrooms, a shooting gallery, and its Pavilion, boasting a huge ballroom and bathhouse on the bay. Those wanting to snack could choose from various coffee shops, a hot dog stand, a bakery, and a teashop.

Its Pavilion, the arrival of the Red Cars, and the completion of a road began an era that brought enormous changes to the peninsula. In 1907, there were only Chance's rental tents and a few scattered cottages, but a mere 15 years later, there were few vacant lots. In a few short years, it had been transformed from a remote and lonely stretch of beach to one of California's most popular playgrounds, featuring rows of cheery, though modest, summer cottages, enticing baubles to buy, and grand entertainment at its stately Pavilion.

Town Takes Shape

In the fall of 1906, the residents of Newport Village (at the base of the pier), West Newport, East Newport, and Balboa voted to incorporate as the City of Newport Beach. The vote was 42 to 12, indicating not only that a large majority supported incorporation, but

Photo Courtesy of Newport Beach Historical Society

Red Cars Arrive at Balboa

also that, despite the large number of bathers playing on its beaches on sunny weekends, there was still an extremely small year-round population in the four communities. Optimistic about the merger, city leaders pledged to join forces to lobby for the creation of a deep, navigable harbor with a safe entrance that would accommodate commercial shipping. Convinced that the City of Newport Beach would not prosper merely as a vacation destination, they envisioned this commercial harbor as the only way to establish a stable, year-round economy in this remote, sparsely-settled town.

In 1907, Newport residents tried once again to convince Washington to survey the bay and to allocate the funds needed to dredge the harbor. They were successful getting the federal government to approve the needed survey, and, for awhile, it looked as if Newport was going to get its long-awaited commercial harbor. At the conclusion of the survey, hope soared when the Army Corps of Engineers proclaimed that a good harbor could be built. Unfortunately, hopes were dashed almost immediately when the Engineers reiterated the government's stance: There must be evidence of substantial already-existing commerce before a harbor would be built using federal funds. According to the 1907 report of the Captain of the Corps of Engineers, **Amos Fries:**

> The ocean commerce of Newport has greatly decreased until at present it consists of occasional cargoes of lumber. There is no shipment out of Newport. All freight is handled over the ocean wharf. . . . In view of the above facts, I am of the opinion that Newport Bay is not worthy of improvement by the General Government at this time.

Residents' laments that commerce could not be established without dredging and jetties fell on deaf ears. To the intense disappointment of these residents, Newport remained trapped in its decades-old vicious circle of needing commerce to warrant bay improvements and being unable to attract this commerce without needed improvements.

With no commercial harbor in sight, Newport was again forced to rely on recreation as its economic base. Hopeful of attracting the rich and famous, Newporters were disappointed when this affluent group selected other locations, like Santa Barbara and Coronado

Sailboat Race in the Bay

Island, as their resorts of choice to play, party, and purchase property. Instead, Newport was forced to rely on the less-affluent Los Angeles and Orange County daytrippers and summer vacationers for its survival. Faced with that reality, residents focused their energies on establishing activities that would appeal to these visitors. Already renowned for its excellent duck hunting and unsurpassed fishing, it was not long before an entirely new sport began to take precedence—recreational boating.

For centuries, boats had been modes of transportation and conveyances for fishermen, but only a few of the richest owned them simply for fun. With the beginning of the 20th century, a fascination with recreational boating was growing – and Newport was one of its most important centers. Soon, yachting equaled the popularity of its numerous duck hunting clubs, with 25 to 30 motorboats, a few recreational sailing yachts, a fleet of sailing skiffs, and over 200 rowboats and canoes dotting the bay. Not unexpectedly, boaters soon wanted to organize. By 1911, the South Coast Yacht Club of Los Angeles, based in Wilmington, voted to allow Newport yachtsmen to organize its first branch, the South Coast Yacht Club, Station A. Not content as a branch of another club, by 1916, Newport boaters organized their own club, the Newport Harbor Yacht Club. A mere seven years later, it had an impressive fleet of 65 boats.

During those early years, the first of a long series of hotly debated issues engulfed the new city: Would it be "wet" and sell liquor, or "dry" by banning all alcoholic beverages? The Women's Christian Temperance Union (WCTU) mounted a powerful battle to ban alcohol, while business battled for a "wet" town, for they knew that Newport's reputation as a playground would quickly fade if it were mandated "dry." Before it became a city in 1906, the sale of alcohol was not permitted. When the City of Newport Beach was incorporated, it was agreed that alcohol could be sold as long as a license was issued. When the WCTU mounted strong opposition to issuing any licenses, a compromise was reached that permitted only one wholesale and one retail license. When both of those licenses were issued in Newport, Balboa Peninsula residents protested strongly. Peninsula businesses complained that there were a suspiciously high number of people heading to Newport each evening for "supplies" and that Newport was also getting all the tourist business. For awhile there was a stalemate. By spring 1907, citizens supporting the sale of alcohol raised $1500 to begin Newport's first newspaper, *Newport News*, established with the single purpose of conducting a campaign for more liquor licenses. It was successful, and soon there were two liquor licenses at Balboa and two at Newport.

The *Newport News*, a 4-page weekly costing $1.50 per year, prospered long after the liquor battle had been settled, fed by a never-ending series of controversies. Established to address a single issue and considered one of the few Democratic newspapers in Orange County, it continued that tradition by devoting a full page each week to politically-motivated editorials, carrying the banner, "A weekly newspaper devoted unreservedly to the advancement of Newport Beach and its harbor." The newspaper struggled and was owned by a variety of publishers for its first 14 years until 1921, when **Sam Meyers** and his wife **Vera** purchased it. Prospering under their leadership, this newspaper played an active role both observing and shaping Newport. In 1957, the Meyers published a rich history of Newport, *50 Golden Years*, comprised of many of the stories of those pivotal years.

52

Shortly before the City of Newport Beach was established, development plans for nearby areas were also being made. Although James Irvine II focused on ranching and agricultural innovation, he did sell some unproductive land. In 1904, he offered 700 acres to **George Hart** for the high price of $150 an acre. Hart immediately made a down payment for the land and laid out a town site that he named Corona del Mar. He knew his town would thrive as soon as the Red Cars arrived, bringing buyers. Unfortunately for him, the Red Cars never reached Corona del Mar, and Hart eventually deeded half of the land back to the Irvines, keeping only his town site, old Corona del Mar.

Bay Island

Recognized as one of the most valuable pieces of real estate in the world, Bay Island is the only natural island in the bay. Halfway up the harbor near the peninsula, it is today a tiny, tree-covered island, bearing magnificent houses surrounded by lovely gardens. Although it was not underwater, it was still only a mud flat with one small hill of dry land when **R. J. Waters** and **Rufus Sanborn** pur-

Photo Courtesy of Newport Harbor Nautical Museum

Bay Island from the Peninsula, 1920s

53

chased it in 1904 for $350. Sanborn, vice president of the Citizens National Bank in Los Angeles, recognized the good duck hunting there and organized a gun club. He built a shack on the dry hill, near today's footbridge, and welcomed hunters. At first these hunters were forced to arrive at low tide and slog through the mud to the island. Soon a walk on pilings was built so that they could arrive anytime and would no longer have to trek through the mud. It was so popular its first year that, by the second year, a poker club was added, and women were invited.

By 1907, Sanborn built the first home on Bay Island. Also in 1907, Sam Tustin (for whom the town of Tustin is named) built the second home on the island and sold it almost immediately to **Madame Helena Modjeska.** Before long, 23 homes had been built and the unique Bay Island Corporation had been established. This corporation still owns all the land on the island. While residents have a continuous lease and own and maintain their homes, the corporation controls the land, maintains the landscaping, and must approve any change in occupancy.

Although she only owned her home on Bay Island for a short time before her death, Helena was Bay Island's most famous early resident. One of 12 children, she was born in Poland in 1840. Her acting talents were quickly recognized, and she was placed under a life contract to the Imperial Theatre of Warsaw. By 1868, she had married a count, **Karol Bozenta Chlapowski**, and became wealthy, as well as acclaimed. She lived a fast-paced life, full of work, travel, and soirees. Eventually her lifestyle, combined with the deaths of her brother and her best friend, overwork, emotional trauma, and tension from constant governmental surveillance, resulted in her physical collapse.

Count Chlapowski had long been fascinated by utopian communities and believed that his wife needed a simpler life. Anaheim, famous as a prosperous colony of German professionals who had successfully adapted to farming, seemed to be the perfect place for them. In 1876, at the height of Helena's fame and recognized as one of Europe's most celebrated stage actresses, the couple journeyed with their friend **Henryk Sienkiewicz**, the author of *Quo Vadis*, to Anaheim

54

to begin new lives as farmers. Seeking a totally different lifestyle, they looked forward to the hard work and simple accommodations.

They were unprepared for the reality of a frontier community without any of Europe's cultural amenities and, even more importantly, without servants. When they arrived, Helena was assigned to be the housekeeper and cook. Totally unskilled and unprepared for the hard work, she failed at her tasks, ached from the unaccustomed work, and was disillusioned and homesick. The Count was equally unsuccessful in accomplishing his assigned tasks and fell into a depression. Hoping that their farming failure had stemmed from unique circumstances at Anaheim, they left and acquired their own farm. The work was still too hard, and she was soon restless, while he continued to be depressed.

By January 1877, they admitted failure. They gave away their farm, and Helena went to San Francisco to hone her English skills in hopes of reviving her career, this time on the American stage. Six months later, she was ready. She was successful and was lovingly embraced by theater lovers across the nation, soon achieving stardom on a par with Sarah Bernhardt. In 1888, they purchased the ranch of friends in Santiago Canyon and planted it with trees and shrubs, calling it "Forest of Arden." Whenever she needed rest, they returned to their canyon retreat. Just before her death in 1909, she bought Tustin's home on Bay Island. As she was famous throughout the world and remembered as one of Orange County's first rich and famous residents, Bay Island for awhile was renamed Modjeska Island in her honor.

Although Bay Island is unique as the bay's only natural island and always its most elegant and exclusive locale, it was just a matter of time and a great deal of dredging before the bay would be dotted by other islands, each with lots for sale to any who had the money.

Balboa Island

As soon as Collins purchased the sandbars that would become Balboa and Lido islands from McFadden, he began to market lots.

Rowboat Rental

The Red Cars brought hundreds of potential buyers whom he took by boat to view his watery home sites. Although some believed his promises and bought, most left without buying. He soon concluded that the promise of dredging was not enough to sell his land. He also concluded that he could not wait for the federal government to pay for the dredging that was needed. Optimistic, entrepreneurial, and undaunted, he began building the dredge that would release his island from the bay's wet clutches. By spring 1906, Collins' small dredge, built in the machine shop on the peninsula, was complete and he was ready to begin dredging a channel opposite Balboa Pavilion. He used this sand and silt to shape his island, now called Balboa Island.

As Balboa Island took shape and home sites emerged from the muck, Collins launched a national advertising campaign. He offered 30 feet by 85 feet inland lots for $600 and charged $750 for lots on the waterfront, using a brochure that also showed an elegant, non-existing hotel at the corner of South Bay and Grand Canal. Cognizant that services were essential, he also promised ferry service, electricity, paved streets, sewers, streetlights, and water.

56

Once he had promised services, Collins began to struggle to provide them. One immediate need was for ferry service and, by 1907, Balboa Island had a ferry, an open launch powered by a single-cylinder engine with a naked piston rod. **Captain John Watts** piloted it across the channel between the peninsula and the island, burning prodigious amounts of oil, with Watts' singing and the clanging of his bell to herald departures.

Although this ferry service was an important step, other services were also desperately needed and, soon, streets were marked, a few flimsy sidewalks were built, and makeshift sewers were constructed. Unfortunately, these sewers poured directly into the bay and washed up onto the "pristine" bathing beaches. Collins also laid out a park in the middle of the island, but it soon disappeared. As money got tight, he subdivided it and sold it as home sites. Even the services that Collins successfully provided, like electricity, were vulnerable. This vulnerability was clearly illustrated when Captain Watts stopped all electricity to the island by taking a bath. He lived in a room on the second floor of the building used to generate all the electricity for the island. Once, when his bathtub overflowed, the generator shorted out, and the island had no electricity for two weeks!

When Collins completed his dredging in 1909 and the lowest lying areas had been filled in to the level of the higher land, most of the island was still submerged at high tide. Collins realized that he needed to build a substantial wall around the island to keep the water out. He compromised by building only a small, 14-inch high wall around the south end only. He also compromised quality by using inexpensive German cement that he had shipped around Cape Horn. As a result of his compromises, for years residents never knew if their homes would be engulfed by the flood tides that surged into the bay with daunting regularity.

Most of the homes in the area were modest summer cottages. One exception was the mansion that Collins built for himself on a small piece of land west of Balboa Island, unsurprisingly named "Collins Island," using the leftover German cement. His cement home was named "Collins Castle" and, although replete with arches, murals, and spectacular gardens, was a great disappointment to its architect who had designed it to be twice as large. This mansion was later purchased by **James Cagney**, in addition to being used by the Coast Guard during World War II. When the castle was destroyed to make room for other homes, its second floor was floated across the bay and became the office for a local tile company.

By 1910, with the dredging done and minimal services installed, Collins was ready to take on another project. He decided to capitalize on California's new-found love of the automobile by constructing an auto speedway around the perimeter of the island and building a 6-car ferry to transport a large number of cars there. Thankfully, Collins lost interest in this project before it was started. When Collins abandoned his plan for an auto speedway, he substituted an equally appalling motorboat speedway around Balboa Island. To encourage that activity, he bought himself a powerboat that roared around Newport Bay, accompanied by sirens, warning nearby swimmers and sailors to get out of its way.

Collins tried to sell Balboa Island as the playground of the rich and famous and focused much advertising on such recreational activities as hunting, fishing, boating, tennis, and horseback riding, followed by gala parties and carnivals. Unfortunately, neither Newport nor Balboa Island was considered fashionable. The rich simply went somewhere else to play. Undependable electricity, water, and gas services and the proliferation of neglected homes did not attract the folks Collins wanted and decidedly concerned those who had bought property. This discouragement impacted lot prices, and they fell to as little as $325 by 1911.

In the face of those daunting problems, Collins continued to promise more and more to lure more buyers. He received some enthusiastic, though not overly factual, publicity from the *Long Beach Press* in this July 25, 1912 article:

> *In the short space of three years, Balboa Island has been built up from a half-submerged lowland in Newport Bay, which at that time was not navigable even for pleasure boats, to a high and dry beach resort. . . . A concrete bulk-*

head, cement sidewalk, costing in the neighborhood of $100,000, has been built around the island to sustain the sand beach on all sides and prevent any possibility of a tidal wave ever infesting the island homes.

Other improvements on Balboa Island consist of permanent sidewalks, sewer, water, gas and electric light connections to every lot. The island also supports a park, which was named Antelpoa in July, and has now been laid out and planted and a new pavilion in the center of the island to cost $10,000 will be constructed in the near future.

Still optimistic, in 1914, Collins planned an extravagant Fourth of July celebration by distributing 8000 brochures across the nation inviting prospective buyers. Thousands came and enjoyed races, tours, food, and parades. When Collins counted all the lots he had sold on Balboa Island since he had begun marketing it, the total was an impressive 700. His hopes were high, and many believed him when he stated that Balboa Island was about to enter its most prosperous era.

Boats and Planes

During those years, visions of transforming the bay into a commercial port remained unfulfilled. Instead, those years brought the Red Cars full of daytrippers. Most came to play, but, as Newport was subdivided and offered for sale, some could afford to stay. These lucky ones bought a lot and built a beach cottage. Many brought a love of water sports with them and, before long, the bay was dotted with sail-, row-, and powerboats on weekends and in the summer.

The affluent still played elsewhere, but, by 1912, things were looking up. Corona del Mar was selected as the setting for a movie, and Balboa Peninsula was in the spotlight when **Glenn Martin** flew from there to Avalon on May 10, 1912. This flight made international news as the longest and fastest over-water flight, and was also the first water landing, for Martin used pontoons to land in the middle of Avalon Harbor. He had been building planes in the old sanctuary of a church at Second and Main in Santa Ana for four years

59

and is credited with constructing the first airplane in the West. According to legend, when Martin went to the bank asking for a small loan to build his first plane, the cashier said, "Young man, you'd better get such foolishness out of your head and settle down and do something useful." One of the founders of Martin Marietta (now Lockheed-Martin), he left an estate of over $14 million when he died in 1955.

Glenn Martin's Flying Machine on the Beach in Avalon

These years offered a glimpse of Newport's future as a tourist destination and a favorite playground for boaters. It was an exciting time full of entrepreneurial developers, Red Cars brimming with tourists, dredges beginning to shape its islands, and even a touch of fame from movies and airplanes. This era began Newport's transformation from swampland and lonely beaches to today's recreational paradise. With waterfront homes selling for as little as $500, Newport was yet to enter its era of affluence, but that, too, was coming. Who would have guessed that less than a century later, the same homes would be selling for millions of dollars?

Island Troubles, Floods, and New Jetty, 1915-1921

When Collins invited 8000 to Balboa Island to celebrate Fourth of July in 1914, few knew that would be Newport's last big bash for five years. The era just before and during World War I was a difficult one, and was marked by floods, debts, and a war that severely reduced the number who came to play. Local optimism about the promise of Newport, as well as smooth-talking promoters with free lunches and deals, disappeared. In their place were disappointed residents facing foreclosure and worried city leaders helplessly watching the bay become a swamp.

The sale of 700 Balboa Island lots did not provide Collins with enough money to install adequate services. Unfortunately, without those services, life on the island was intolerable. Despite his continuing optimism and promises, buyers slowly began to realize that Collins was incapable of addressing their needs. The foreclosure signs that began to appear in 1914 were the first disturbing signs of bad times to come. Soon, sales came to a halt while Collins' debts continued to mount until, in 1915, he lost all of his Newport holdings, with the exception of his mansion on Collins Island. That signaled the end of the boom, and depression took hold of the island.

Balboa Island residents were stuck with an inadequate, crumbling seawall and homes that were flooded with disturbing regularity. Sewage continued to wash up on to their beaches before flowing out of the bay. Additionally, they had no water: Collins had collected money for it from buyers but had never paid the city. As conditions on the island got increasingly untenable, owners gave up their land for practically nothing. Property values plummeted until many lots were acquired by simply paying back taxes. In 1918, 12 lots were sold for a total of $300.

During those desperate times, the only solution seemed to be to forfeit its independence and, in 1916, Balboa Island was officially annexed by the City of Newport Beach. The purpose of the annexation was to get water and other services to the island. Unfortunately, the merger also brought taxes, something Collins had promised buyers they would never have to pay, and many did not celebrate annexation to the city. Initially, no one had anything to celebrate, for the situation got steadily worse. Ferry service was discontinued, and water and gas interruptions continued to plague the island—even after owners had paid taxes for these services!

Finally, in 1918, when conditions had become unbearable, the Balboa Island Improvement Association was established to address the problems. Hope began to revive when, in 1919, the association organized a large meeting and a Fourth of July celebration. That meeting resulted in the approval of a long list of needed improvements. Topping this list was the repair of the inadequate seawall. Others were dependable ferry service, a functional sewer system, an adequate water supply, streetlights, paving of certain streets, and burying gas and water lines so that fishing boats would not continually cut them.

Although the list was daunting, the optimistic neighborhood association began to devise plans to address each of the problems. Its first step was to form a committee to meet with the mayor to get his support. Unfortunately, that meeting did not go well. He was unsympathetic and told them, "The island is a dump. It was sold by a lot of damn crooks and bought by a lot of damn fools." Despite that hurtful rebuff, the formation of the Balboa Island Improvement Association marked the beginning of the island's tradition of proactive citizen involvement that eventually transformed it into an exclusive residential neighborhood for some and a tourist destination for many.

Balboa Island was not alone in its troubles. When Collins was losing Balboa Island in 1915, Corona del Mar was also failing. Despite over a decade of active advertisement and promotion, there were only 15 homes and one modest, small hotel. Additionally, the City of

Newport Beach faced financial problems that were so serious that bankruptcy threatened it.

Silt and Floodwaters

On top of financial problems, natural forces were also threatening Newport's vibrancy—silt and debris were rapidly filling in the bay. During those years, the Santa Ana River entered a flood plain between Newport and Huntington Beaches before flowing into the bay. While in the flood plain, the river broke up into many small channels. Initially, these channels were full of willows and vines that sieved the silt from the water. But as farmers and ranchers settled the area, the willows and vines were cut, and the small channels in which the Santa Ana had deposited its silt were cleared and drained so that the silt-laden water began to flow directly into the bay. Additionally, a 300-foot channel was built to contain the Santa Ana and to control flooding. This channel, carrying silt and debris, emptied directly into the west end of Newport Bay and, combined with the clearing of the silt-catching vines and willows, resulted in a badly silted bay.

A series of floods made Newport's financial and geographical challenges even more daunting. For several years, winter rainstorms brought raging waters that flooded homes, damaged roofs, and further complicated the service problems throughout the area by breaking gas and water mains. One of the most memorable of these floods hit Newport in January 1916, when the levees along the Santa Ana River broke, freeing the river to hurl a rapidly-moving maelstrom of debris, silt, and water toward Newport. As it approached, it became clear that Newport would be destroyed unless the raging river could escape to the ocean before it engulfed the city. Several brave, quick-thinking citizens took matters into their hands. Without permission, they took a Pacific Electric Red Car and drove it to a low lying area between Newport and Huntington Beach. They then frantically began digging a channel under the Southern Pacific rails at the edge of the ocean in hope that the river would empty into the ocean there, rather than flowing through Newport. It worked! The river broke through and hurled its tons of debris into the ocean, taking a quarter-mile of railroad tracks with it. Fearful of reprisals from the Southern Pacific Railroad for the rail damage caused by digging this channel, it was many years before anyone talked about what really happened the night Newport was saved. At age 82, one of these men, **George Morales,** recalled saving Newport:

> *A P.E. car was standing on the tracks at Balboa and we took the car and went as far as we could beyond West Newport when [we] opened the railroad bank and let the water into the ocean. That sure saved Newport. We never said much about it because we were scared lest the railroad get after us.*

Despite that daring rescue, Newport was still damaged, as the channel did not divert all of the floodwater and, for days, the area was littered with dead animals, debris, trees, and thousands of oranges. Nevertheless, many believe that the heroic actions of these men saved Newport.

Fire and Flu

The McFaddens' lumber business had been most successful, and virtually all Newport buildings were constructed of wood. With the real threat of fire, forward-looking citizens organized a volunteer fire department. The first editor of the *Newport News* was appointed Fire Chief and given a salary of $10 per month. By 1910, the Fire Department had acquired three hose reels and a lot on Newport Boulevard to store their equipment. Four years later, a large wooden garage had been built on the lot to store its increasing supply of firefighting equipment, including helmets, slickers, and two hand-pumper trucks. Ironically, this wooden garage was the scene of Newport's first fire. Not only was the garage ruined, but all of Newport's firefighting equipment was destroyed before it could be employed.

In 1917, Dr. Conrad Richter arrived in Newport Beach with his bride. He had just retired as a ship's surgeon and envisioned a relaxing retirement rich with the recreational activities that abounded at his new home. He was wrong, for he had barely begun to enjoy his retirement before the devastating 1919 flu epidemic that swept the world threatened the health of Newporters. As there was no physician in the area, Dr. Richter went to work, driving a Model "T" Ford around the town calling on the ill. He found an assistant, and they worked together saving the lives of those stricken by the flu. They were so successful that only one died from the deadly flu epidemic. He eventually opened two offices, one in Newport and one in Balboa.

Despite his services, it soon became clear that the hospital in Santa Ana was too far away to handle emergencies and, by 1925, a drive was launched to fund a hospital in Newport. It was successful, and within a few short years Newporters celebrated the opening of its own hospital at 9th and Balboa Boulevard, equipped with five beds, three treatment rooms, and an operating room.

Dredging Brings Hopes

Luckily for Newport, in June 1915, the California Legislature passed a law allowing cities and counties to bond themselves for reclamation projects, and a bond measure to fund one jetty at the mouth of the bay was immediately put on the Orange County ballot. Dreams of a commercial seaport were revived, as bond campaigners promised its approval would attract industry. It passed in September 1916, and, a year later, 5000 enthusiastic onlookers gathered to cheer the placement of the first rock in the jetty. The bond only provided enough money for one jetty, not the two that were needed, but citizens were confident that the federal government would recognize Newport's commercial promise and fund the second jetty as soon as the first was completed.

Despite this progress, the Santa Ana River continued to threaten floods as well as depositing silt and debris into the bay. Clearly, something had to be done to tame the river if the bay were to remain navigable, much less a deep-sea port. In 1919, another $500,000 Orange County bond was proposed to build Bitter Point

Dam to divert the Santa Ana River from Newport Bay, lengthen the recently completed west jetty to 1900 feet, dredge, and build a wharf and railroad spur. Although the project was estimated at $635,000, only $500,000 was budgeted, for it was assumed that the dredged silt and debris could be sold for $135,000 to bridge the funding gap. It was approved, and Newporters celebrated with their first water carnival, including a naval band, airplanes buzzing overhead, a bathing beauty contest, Sub Chaser #307 chugging up the channel, and free motion pictures.

Celebration of First Rock Placed in Jetty, 1917

Although the Santa Ana River was diverted to the Pacific Ocean when the Bitter Point Dam was completed in 1921, the rest of the project was plagued with difficulties. Work was delayed in the summer of 1920 when the dredge burned. Then, heavy summer seas swept sands from beneath the new jetty with such force it began to sink. An additional $50,000 had to be allocated to cover the cost of these repairs. Also, anticipated sales of the dredged materials did not materialize, as no one wanted to purchase the smelly muck. The Irvines were the only ones to buy it, leaving a large gap between real and budgeted costs of the project, plus a mountain of unsold foul-smelling silt and debris. As a result of the unanticipated budget gap, the wharf and railroad spur were never built on a strip of bayfront land that had been donated by Irvine in 1921. Instead, the lot later became the site of the Balboa Bay Club and the Sea Scout Base.

In light of the bond-funded improvements, many believed that federal funding would soon follow. Ever optimistic, Newporters went to Washington to plead for funds once again. This time they had some success. In 1917, Congress approved funding to dredge the bay to conform to the lines identified by a survey four years earlier. This dredging established the shape of Newport's harbor, and, despite the pleas of those whose land was still underwater, rendered the land that was still submerged undevelopable. The establishment of harbor lines was an important step toward establishing the bay, but it was only one small step in a decades-long battle against the silt that continued to threaten it.

Workmen Placing Rocks in Jetty

Despite difficult years marked by bankruptcy, flood, fire, flu, and war, Newport made great progress by the organization of a strong Balboa Island Improvement Association dedicated to addressing the island's problems, establishment of a volunteer fire department and medical services, and significant bay improvements, including a jetty, a dredged channel, and a diverted Santa Ana River that would no longer dump silt into the bay. And, probably most importantly, Newport had gained the ability to raise money to address its needs through bonds. Although difficult and frightening for those who had invested all of their money in the promise of Newport, these years set the stage for Newport's next chapter—jetty expansion and the race against silt.

Main Street, Balboa

The Race against Silt,
1922-1928

Much of the Newport Bay people enjoy today is the combination of a fluke of nature and an enormous amount of expensive dredging. Between 1906, when Collins first took his small dredge into the channel, and 1921, $1.5 million had been spent. Although, in retrospect, the work had hardly begun, those who envisioned a commercial seaport were sure this dredging was enough to lure ships and industry to the bay. They were wrong and many, especially those in Newport, were bitterly disappointed. On the other hand, residents of Balboa were relieved that industry was not ruining their water wonderland. After an undercurrent of dissention for decades, during the 1920s, a division within the City of Newport Beach grew, with Newport residents actively supporting commercial development and Balboa residents fighting it.

When Newport and Balboa merged in 1906, city leaders from both areas had pledged to transform Newport into a commercial harbor. While residents of Newport continued to support this vision, those of Balboa gradually realized that they loved their city just as it was. They were pleased that they were attracting more and more visitors, and believed that the area could prosper as a tourist destination. As plans for a deep-sea harbor continued, they became concerned that industry would destroy the charm of their city. By November 1923, the battle lines were drawn when an important commercial opportunity, an oil pipeline, was proposed. According to the November 18, 1923 *Long Beach Press:*

> *On Tuesday the voters of Newport Beach, which comprises the two communities on the Newport harbor peninsula, will go to the polls to decide whether a franchise granted by the board of trustees of the city to operate a pipeline and filling station for oil tankers on the pier at Newport shall become effective or void.*

69

The fight has become most bitter, and now the people of the town of Newport Beach are lined up almost solidly behind the proposition, while those residing at Balboa, which is primarily a resort settlement, are as bitterly opposed. . . .

The proponents of the proposition declare that if Newport is ever to become a harbor, it must start some time and they declare that there is no better time than the present, with the shipment of oil as a beginning. . . .

On the other hand, the people of Balboa are just as set in their ideas against the granting of the franchise. They claim that waste oil will spoil the beach for bathing. They point to the fact that the beach at Balboa and Newport is the only one within a radius of fifty miles of Los Angeles that has not been commercialized or which is not having difficulty with oil washing up on the shore. "There are no black streaks in the sand here, and we want to keep it that way if we possibly can."

Three days later, the *Long Beach Press* added:

One of the hottest elections ever held in Newport Beach Tuesday resulted in a victory for the commercial development of Newport harbor when the people voted a majority of 91 in favor of a pipeline franchise and pier lease.

Although the oil franchise was approved, Newport did not attract the industry it needed to become a commercial center. Visionary entrepreneurs with money and ideas were simply not drawn to Newport; instead, they selected other promising California cities in which to invest their resources and energies. Nor had Newport begun to attract wealthy millionaires, like William Wrigley, who purchased Catalina Island, or William Randolph Hearst, who built his castle at San Simeon. Instead, Newport Beach seemed destined to remain a weekend and summer escape for city-weary workers who built modest beach cottages. Newport residents, discontented with this destiny and intent on replacing its modest cottages with prosperous industries, were unable to envision the recreational paradise Newport Beach would become.

Despite their disagreement about the future of Newport Beach, residents of Balboa and Newport would all have been appalled if they had realized the amount of money that would be needed to develop the bay. Despite the $1.5 million that had been spent, the work had barely begun. The west jetty was neither high nor long enough to protect boats entering the channel, and an east jetty was desparately needed. Additionally, the sandbar at the entrance was growing rapidly, and the channel in the bay was silting up before the dredging had even been completed.

Balboa Island and the Ferry

Despite the enormous amounts of dredging still needed, Balboa Island was entering better times. Much of the credit for this belongs to the success of the Balboa Island Improvement Association. This active neighborhood association spearheaded a number of improvements that made the island livable, including completion of a sewer system, paving and lighting of streets, and construction of several public piers. A significant battle was won in 1924, when a zoning ordinance barring a fish cannery was approved. Not only did the ordinance firmly establish Balboa Island as a residential community, it was also the first time that recreational and residential interests defeated the commercial development that had been sought for so many decades.

Equal in importance to those improvements was the establishment of dependable and inexpensive ferry service to the island. Although service had stopped when the island merged with the City of Newport Beach, in 1919, **Joseph Allan Beek** had taken over the defunct ferry business. Beek had fallen in love with the area in 1907, when he was a student in Los Angeles, and spent the rest of his life being one of its most enthusiastic and persuasive boosters, proclaiming to all that he would rather live there in a cottage than in a mansion anywhere else. He immediately reduced fares from 10 to 5 cents, and put a canopied launch not much larger than a rowboat into service. Named *Islander*, it had been wrecked and abandoned at the harbor entrance until Beek rescued and restored it. Despite cut-

71

Photo Courtesy of Newport Harbor Nautical Museum

Beek's Pier with Facilities for the Race Committee

ting his rates in half, he prospered and, by 1922, was able to expand his ferry fleet by acquiring the *Fat Ferry*, a 22-foot, 20-passenger barge pushed by a launch and capable of carrying one auto. Three years later, he expanded his fleet again by adding two more auto ferries, each capable of carrying three cars.

In 1920, Beek was also hired as Newport's first Harbormaster, at a salary of $25 a month. One of his first challenges as Harbormaster was to mark the often-shifting channel. As neither the city nor county would provide the buoys he needed, he made his own out of two washtubs fastened together and painted black and white. Fondly called "Joe Beek's hat boxes," he eventually got $300 from the City Council to pay for them, in addition to getting their permission to "clutter up our channel with these contraptions to his heart's content." Constantly striving to improve the safety of the bay, by 1923, he had also been successful getting a bell buoy installed off the jetty. Beek continued to play a major role in Newport throughout his life, balancing multiple careers, including operating his ferry service, managing a Balboa Island real estate business, teaching Newport's youth to sail, serving as Secretary of the California Senate, and, as

72

Chairman of the Citizen's Harbor Committee, he even helped dredge the channel in 1928, when silt threatened to choke it once again.

As Balboa Island got its sewers, lights, roads, and a dependable ferry service, foreclosure signs disappeared, land values rose, and sales increased dramatically. By 1923, lots that could not be sold for $25 in 1919 were selling for $200 to $300. By 1929, the same lots were selling for $700 to $800 and some prime waterfront lots were selling for as much as $4000. Prices on the island continued to increase until inside lots sold for $1000 in 1940, while waterfront lots brought $5000. By 1956, these inside lots were selling for $12,000, and waterfront lots for $25,000 to $30,000. Before long, there were no more lots to sell on Balboa Island, as cottages covered the entire island.

In the Spotlight

Although Newport did not attract industry, it attracted ever-increasing numbers of visitors, who chose Newport as their favorite place to play. As a large proportion of those who came to play owned boats,

Aerial Photo of Balboa Island, 1933

boating soon became Newport's number one pastime. By 1923, the Newport Harbor Yacht Club was joined by other clubs, including the Southland Sailing Club (eventually renamed the Balboa Yacht Club) and the Balboa Island Yacht Club which taught youngsters between the ages of 4 and 16 the joys of sailing. Located on the beach in front of Beek's home, this latter club taught many of Newport's future yachtsmen to sail. In 1922, residents were pleased when Newport was selected as the location for the Southern California Yachting Association Regatta. The entire town welcomed the 200 boaters who came and cheered the 66 boats that raced. Although hopes for Newport's commercial dominance died hard, the money these boaters spent sewed the early seeds of a new dream —an economy based on clean industries—boating and tourism.

In addition to boating, Newport was thrilled to welcome **Duke Kahanamoku**, the famous Olympic champion, Hollywood actor, Hawaiian folk hero, and world-renowned surfer. Recipient of numerous swimming honors, he came to California not only to swim, but also to demonstrate the new sport that was sweeping California's beaches, surfing. He was so impressed with its surf that he headquartered his surfing club, rumored to be the largest in the world, at Corona del Mar. Considered the king of water sports until he was bested in the 1924 Paris Olympics by 20-year old Johnny Weissmuller, the genial Duke helped solidify Newport's reputation as a recreational center.

The 1920s also put Newport in the spotlight, for its stunning geography provided the perfect location for movies. Blessed with calm bay waters, crashing surf, empty beaches, cliffs, and lots of sunshine, it provided a backdrop that filmmakers sought. For awhile it was the favored location for comedies. By 1916, Keystone Comedies had left their crowded Santa Monica beach location for Newport, and comedians Max Sennett and Fatty Arbuckle were cavorting in one of their 100 short movies filmed in the area. Also in 1916, Douglas Fairbanks filmed a beach comedy there, and, in 1921, "Buster" Keaton starred in the first of his many Newport-based comedies.

Not only comedies were filmed at Newport. It was also the location for such adventures as *The Three Musketeers, The Count of Monte*

Cristo, Captain Blood, and *The Sea Hawk,* many of which used local fishermen as extras for the swimming stunts, while Corona del Mar became the setting of *Tarzan* movies. Also, *Cleopatra,* called "the most sumptuous and magnificent production yet conceived," temporarily transformed Newport's upper bay into the Nile with costumed warriors battling on barges. The filming was not without incident. Someone stole one of Cleopatra's costumes from the set, but she still had 49 others, and the show went on.

Newport's time as a movie location was short-lived, and its decade in the spotlight ended when others discovered its perfect location. As its reputation as a playground grew, its appeal as a movie location diminished until, by 1931, Newport had too many homes and utility poles to shoot the exotic scenes needed for Hollywood's movies. Filmmakers sought a new location and many of them selected Catalina Island just 40 miles off Newport's shores.

Dangerous Channel

Although boating was thriving in the bay, the entrance to the harbor was becoming increasingly unsafe. As Newport sought to solidify its reputation as a water wonderland, all knew that its dangerous channel posed a serious problem. How could it lure boaters to Newport when only the bravest visiting yachtsmen dared to enter its challenging and ever-shifting entrance? When three drowned in a 1923 New Year's Day accident, **Antar Deraga**, a Russian-born meteorologist who was in charge of the lights and flags at the entrance, started the Life Saving Corps. Although the Corps saved many lives, the entrance still claimed too many. In June 1924, when a fishing launch capsized, the Corps worked for hours to resuscitate its 12 passengers. Their fine work saved four, but eight died in the tragic accident.

Already dangerous, the entrance became even more dangerous when, in May 1925, **Muriel**, a ship that had been used for movies but was later converted to a mackerel barge, got stuck and sank inside the entrance. Despite all attempts at removal, she remained there for five years, creating an additional hazard to all who braved

75

the dangerous entrance. In addition to the hazard that she created at the entrance, she made the news with a suspiciously dramatic tale of Captain Eliason's battle with her new occupants, reported in the July 1, 1927 *Press-Telegram:*

> *[He] won a two-hour gruesome battle with a fifteen-foot octopus deep in the water-filled hold of the old three-masted ship Muriel, aground in the entrance of Newport Harbor. Today a corps of armed divers is to search the hold for another larger octopus and a group of four or five smaller octopi seen by Eliason.*
>
> *Diver Eliason was making an inspection of the ship's hull when he found himself grasped by a tentacle. The next instant he was battling in water filled with inky fluid as tentacle after tentacle wrapped around his legs and body. Round and round they threshed while Eliason's assistant continued to turn the handle of the pump which meant life to the diver, while from time to time he tried to signal for help to workmen on the nearby jetty. There were times during the two-hour struggle when the octopus almost had the best of the diver. Marks of his tentacles are visible today.*
>
> *He does not know how it happened but finally, struggling to tear the tentacles loose with one bare hand while he punched about with the hammer in the other, he loosened the creature's grip. Thinking it was dead, he started up the ladder.*
>
> *Then the battle began all over again, with the diver just beneath the surface, clinging to the ladder with one hand, and the octopus clinging to the diver and the ladder with all the vigor it had. Here Eliason's assistant managed to summon another workman, who caught hold of Eliason and by the combined efforts of the two tore the grip of the octopus loose and hauled both diver and sea monster to the deck of the vessel, where it was dispatched with a blow between the eyes.*
>
> *Octopi are rarely encountered in Southern California waters, and then only in some sequestered hole or cave in a rocky coast where the surroundings are much like those of the hold of the Muriel, which ran aground two years ago. No octopi as large as the fifteen-foot monster killed by Eliason have been recorded in Southern California.*

76

Hull of the *Muriel*, High and Dry

One of the most dramatic of the accidents at the entrance to Newport Bay occurred in June 1925. Surfer Duke Kahanamoku watched a 40-foot fishing boat, *Thelma*, trying to enter the harbor in conditions that were too dangerous for a safe entry. He tried frantically to get the captain to turn around. Instead, the captain waited for a lull and tried to speed through the treacherous entrance. The *Thelma* capsized, tossing all 17 passengers overboard. Duke grabbed his long mahogany surfboard and, by making three trips, saved seven who were flailing helplessly in the surf. Other surfers joined Duke in the rescue effort and were able save another five. According to a June 15, 1925 account in the *Los Angeles Times*:

> The swell, as it gained momentum, merged into a mountainous wave and crashed over the bow, smashing through the heavy plate glass of the engine-room flooding the compartment and stopping the engine.
>
> Practically all the members of the pleasure party were swept overboard with the first wave and were struggling in the midst of the torn wreckage and pounding waves. Another wave quickly followed in the wake of the first,

swept the boat its entire length, sending rigging overboard into a maelstrom of confusion and pitched the boat on its side. . . . Before the fishermen could put on life preservers or assistance could reach them, the small boat was caught broadside in the teeth of three tremendous breakers and rolled completely over three times.

Encumbered by heavy clothing, the fishermen were thrown from the boat and started to sink almost immediately. Only a few were able to reach the upturned craft and cling safely to the keel.

Battling with his surfboard through heavy seas in which no small boat could live, Kahanamoku was the first to reach the drowning men. He made three successive trips to the beach and carried four victims the first trip, three the second, and one the third.

According to Captain Porter, "The Duke's performance was the most superhuman rescue act and the finest display of surfboard riding that has ever been seen in the world, I believe."

Despite lauding the heroic rescue, Newporters mourned the victims claimed at the entrance and knew that such deadly accidents occurred far too often. Not only was the entrance a hazard for boaters, but it was also a severe liability to the continued economic prosperity of Newport. Industry would never select Newport, and even yachters would avoid the bay if it remained so dauntingly dangerous to enter. Motivated by too many tragic deaths and fears for Newport's economic vitality, the push for harbor improvements began once again.

Jetties

Although the debate between commercial and recreational development continued to rage, both sides agreed that, until a large amount of money was sunk into the bay, neither group would get what it wanted. By 1926, less than 10 years after its first major dredging, the channel had silted up so badly that, at low tide, the entrance was only 4 feet deep and was impossible to enter except at high tide.

Hope for more federal funding was dim—as Washington appeared to have concluded that bay improvements would not serve the nation, but would only enrich property owners. With no other options, locals finally recognized that they would have to fund the improvements themselves.

In 1926, a county harbor improvement bond for $1.2 million was proposed. Although backers fought valiantly to gather enough votes, it was defeated, as was a smaller bond proposed later the same year. Those failures posed a tremendous problem for Newport as it was becoming a world-class yachting center. Having been selected to host two important yachting events in 1928, the start of the Transpac Race and the International Star Regatta, residents saw their silted channel as a disaster in the making. Something had to be done . . . quickly. By February 1927, residents took matters into their own hands and approved a $500,000 city bond for a 1500-foot east jetty, another extension (900 feet this time) to the still-inadequate west jetty, and more dredging.

The project was far more difficult than envisioned. Believing that the Army Corps of Engineers would do the work, residents were

Celebrating the 1927 Jetty Repair

concerned when the Newport city engineer was hired to complete the project on commission. Their concern was well-founded—the extension to the western jetty was designed to curve. Unfortunately, this curve pushed the surf to the west and residents watched in horror as this diverted surf eroded oceanfront property and undermined the foundations of beachfront homes along two entire blocks. In panic, they frantically dumped carloads of rock into the ocean to build rock groins to protect homes and stop the rampant erosion. Although the rock groins successfully protected the oceanfront, they cost an unbudgeted $200,000 and required the approval of another bond. The eastern jetty did not pose as many problems, but money was scarce by that time, and it was constructed of concrete rather than rock.

With all the money spent and huge amounts of dredging still needed, residents watched helplessly as sand, deposited at the east side of the entry to form a beach at Corona del Mar, was immediately washed back into the channel. Additionally, breakers eroded Balboa beach, and the channel sandbar grew and grew. To make matters worse, the dredge was caught in swells, snapped its moorings, and landed in the mud. Extensively damaged, it had to be towed to Long Beach, adding even more unbudgeted expense to the disaster-plagued project.

As the summer of 1928 approached, it looked as if the season, anticipated as one of Newport's grandest, would be a disaster. While citizens prepared for the influx of racers by building a new ballroom, the Rendezvous, and offering luxurious home sites for sale, city officials braced themselves for a dreadful, embarrassing summer. To avert the looming crisis, local businessmen and yachtsmen intervened.

Joe Beek temporarily gave up his position as Harbormaster to serve as the full-time Chairman of the 15-member Citizens' Harbor Committee. Although some members of the committee wanted to continue to try to get the government to fund the dredging, the majority decided that route was hopeless and that funds must be raised locally. Beek began raising funds by seeking donations from everyone, even pennies and nickels from Newport's children. The committee rented a small 6-inch dredge not designed for ocean work, affectionately known as *Little Aggie*, and hired dredgers who promised to complete the project for $10,000, $1000 of which they would contribute if the committee raised the remaining $9000.

The committee successfully raised the needed funds and *Little Aggie* began slowly deepening the channel, inching her way toward the ocean. Beek worked alongside in his boat, *Vamos*, a 30-foot cruiser used as a race committee boat. He sounded the channel ahead of *Little Aggie* and repeatedly towed her back into the bay when her moorings broke and she began drifting to sea. Committee members also volunteered their time to this dredging project. Although blessed with good weather that winter of 1927-28, there were still many times when it looked as if the strong currents and southeast winds, with extreme winter tides, would destroy *Little Aggie.*

Amazingly, *Little Aggie* reached the end of the channel by the starting date of the Transpac on Memorial Day. Citizens breathed a collective sigh of relief, celebrated their 100-foot wide, 10-foot deep channel, and prepared to welcome the world to their wonderful harbor. That summer, not only did Newport successfully host the Transpac, but it also welcomed thousands of Star owners from all

Joe Beek's *Vamos* and Star Raceboat

over the world and helped Duke Kahanamoku's Surfing Club host the Surfboard Championships of the World.

Citizens could congratulate themselves. For a mere $10,453 ($1000 of which had been contributed by the dredgers), they had averted disaster and had been the perfect host to boaters and surfers from around the world. That summer catapulted Newport into the limelight as a world-class yachting center. Incidentally, citizens also hired themselves a new city engineer, the former engineer having been fired because of the curved-jetty fiasco.

Despite these successes, Newport citizens still faced a few more difficult years. The harbor projects had added a heavy tax burden, while other needed services, such as streets, sewers, sidewalks, and bridges, languished in need of repair. Patient and resilient, Newporters stoically bore these inconveniences and focused on repaying their mounting debts.

Lido Isle

In 1923, **W. K. Parkinson,** an oil millionaire, bought the land that would become Lido Isle for $45,000. He had made his millions through a unique turn of events. In 1911, he had given a friend money to homestead cheap government land around Maricopa, with the understanding that they would split the 160 acres equally between them. Parkinson requested the half with the home and the stream. Without telling him, his friend switched the parcels so that Parkinson was deeded the land without the stream and home. As it turned out, the joke was on his friend, for multi-million dollar oil deposits were discovered on Parkinson's half. Amazingly, the oil stopped at the property line and his friend got nothing but land with a home and a stream.

Parkinson expended another $261,000 dredging the bay and filling in the swampy land until, by 1924, Lido Isle was an impressive 11 feet above high tide level. Swampy no longer, Lido Isle instantly became an intriguing investment to real estate entrepreneurs. In 1926, he was offered a whopping $750,000 for Lido Isle—but

Dredge, off Lido Isle, mid-1920s

refused to sell. He held out for a better offer. After his death in 1927, his widow sold to **William Clark Crittenden**, a San Francisco promoter, who offered $1.25 million but paid only $50,000—for the promised payments were never made.

Crittenden planned to subdivide and sell Lido Isle as an exclusive neighborhood of luxurious mansions. And he knew exactly who could help him design it—**Franz Herding**, a renowned Swiss architect who was familiar with villa designs on the Riviera of France and Italy. Herding designed a lovely Mediterranean-style community with walled gardens named for the exclusive Italian Adriatic resort.

Once planning was completed, temporary utilities were installed, and construction of six model homes began. Bay front lots were offered for sale, with asking prices beginning at $6200, but few were buying.

With few sales, Crittenden did not pay Parkinson's widow. She turned her finances over to her attorney, expecting that he would be able to get the money Crittenden owed her. Instead, he absconded with her entire fortune. Although he was eventually disbarred, it is

83

unlikely that Parkinson's estate ever received any more than the initial $50,000 down payment from Crittenden.

Despite lagging sales, 1928 brought an important victory to Lido Isle. For years before his death, Parkinson had been trying to get a permit from the Army Corps of Engineers to build a bridge from Lido Isle to the mainland. The permit was finally granted, and completion of this bridge in July 1928 was celebrated with fanfare. Lido Isle was now easily accessible, ready to be subdivided and sold.

Rumrunners' Paradise

The Prohibition Years, 1919-1933, found Newport a convenient distribution point for rumrunners and a great place to dance, drink, and gamble. During those years, Balboa Peninsula became known for its dance halls, where big bands could be heard; games of chance played; and bootleg liquor flowed. Previously quiet during the winters, in those years it gained renown as a lively year-round place to play.

One of the reasons that illegal whiskey flowed so freely in Newport was its role as a convenient entry point for rumrunners. During those years, rumrunners in black-hulled speedboats easily smuggled whiskey into Newport from both Canada and Mexico. Often using Catalina Island as a secret storage spot, they waited in the midnight waters until watchers on shore used powerful lights to flash a "coast clear" signal. As soon as they received the signal, they would speed to the beaches of Newport, where liquor was unloaded and spirited away to Southern California speakeasies.

Authorities occasionally intervened. When they did, bottles of whiskey were smashed and flowed down the City Hall driveway and into the drain, while onlookers watched in horror. To many Newporters, enjoying a bit of whiskey was simply not a criminal offense. Some were even glad to participate in hijinks designed to circumvent a law they considered ridiculous. Once, when the Marshal, who had just confiscated six cases of rum, was called to an emergency, the City Clerk stole it to protect it from being smashed. When the clerk also was called away, the six cases disappeared into

84

the back of a local's car. The *Newport News* characterized this inability of many residents to take the crime of rumrunning seriously in its July 27, 1923 editorial:

> *Reading the scare lines in the city dailies of rumrunners, snooping around Newport, of the mysterious night signaling, of revenue cutters—hundreds of 'em—of greasy sea serpents oozing through the brine—ain't it awful, Mabel? A feller would think a gang of pirates infested Balboa Island.*

During the first three decades of the 20th century, Newport lost its last vestiges of isolation. Not only was Corona del Mar annexed in 1924, but three years later Newport was connected to other towns when the Coast Highway was completed. When Mary Pickford and her husband, Douglas Fairbanks, dedicated the completion of that important highway by tying the ribbon that symbolized the connection between Newport and growing settlements to the south, Newporters knew that their city was entering the mainstream of Southern California coastal life.

In a few short decades, both Lido Isle and Balboa Island had become residential communities; the battle against silt was being won; and the growing city had finally gotten its desperately needed jetties. Newport's reputation as a playground was established, and its appeal as a world-class yachting center was growing. Although residents still had some serious battles to win, those years transformed a small, swampy stretch of beach into a popular destination for tourists and discerning yachtsmen from around the world. No longer comprised of miles of lonely beaches and marshland, Newport was soon to become one of California's most popular destinations.

Bay Avenue in 1916

Looking toward Balboa Island from Pavilion, 1932

Great Depression Brings Victories, 1929-1938

The Stock Market Crash of 1929 plunged the United States into an economic depression that stunned the young, exuberant nation. Despite this national shock, the first few years of the Depression seemed to have little effect if one believes optimistic newspaper articles. On December 31, 1930 the *Press-Telegram* enthusiastically reported:

> *The 1930 season saw no depression in the Newport Harbor section. A new $200,000 harbor improvement was completed; a new $410,000 high school plant was built on a fine 25-acre site in Newport Heights; a record-breaking $1,700,000 improvement project was completed on Lido Isle; and modern development enterprises were consummated in West Newport, El Bayo Balboa Tract, and in other sections of the city. Building for 11 months of 1930 was $164,105 – greater than for the 12 months of 1929, which was $117,685 greater than 1928.*

The good news continued with the January 28, 1932 *Press-Telegram*:

> *The Newport Bay communities, in spite of the ups and downs of Wall Street in the last two years, have seen their greatest advancement in that same time. More building, real estate sales, homes, all-year residents, yachts, and other pleasure craft in the improved harbor, school facilities, better highways, and transportation facilities – more of all things that make life worthwhile is the story of the Newport-Balboa area in the last two years.*

Despite those optimistic articles, many Newport residents struggled, as did citizens in the rest of the nation. Before long, fishing boats lay idle; "For Sale" signs appeared as homeowners faced foreclosure; and fewer visitors came to play and spend. Nevertheless, the brunt of the Depression did not cripple Newport as it did other parts of the nation and, for many, those years are fondly remembered. Not only did they bring the developement of Lido Isle and the arrival of Newport's first Hollywood stars—they also brought long-awaited federally-funded bay improvements.

Lido Isle Trials

Although the completion of the bridge between Lido and the mainland was celebrated with fanfare in 1928, this sandbar-turned-island still had a long way to go to become the elegant residential community envisioned by Crittenden. Although he had installed temporary utilities and built model homes, buyers were not interested in the bayfront lots he was offering for $6200.

In desperation, Crittenden went to the city with a proposal: If Newport would build streets and install permanent utilities, he would fund the improvements by charging extra for each lot. Despite the already-overburdened city coffers and serious concerns by city officials who knew that Lido lots were not selling, his proposal was eventually approved. By 1930, a contract to install underground utilities, streetlights, streets, and curbs was awarded to the Griffith Company. Totaling $1.23 million, this contract set a record as the largest of its kind in California.

Unfortunately, lot sales still lagged, and, later that year, Crittenden was forced to relinquish his Lido holdings. When the ownership of 105 acres of Lido Isle reverted to Title Insurance and Trust of Los Angeles, the company moved fast to recover its losses. A tent on the sand was erected, and lots were offered at a fraction of their former asking price. By July 1931, $500,000 had been recovered. Unfortunately, most of Lido remained unsold. By 1932, many lots were abandoned, and some of the 38 homes on Lido were for sale.

Needless to say, the lagging lot sales did not generate enough revenue to fund the Griffith Company contract. In exchange, the company accepted 750 Lido home sites instead of the contracted cash, leaving the Title Company with just over 100 lots left to liquidate. Serious about getting rid of Lido lots as quickly as possible, in 1935, the two owners, Title Insurance and Griffith Company, gave **Paul Palmer** an exclusive contract to sell them. Passionate, persuasive, and confident, he began energetically marketing his lots, determined to ignore the foreclosure signs dotting the island. Convinced that he would sell everything within five years, he would have been appalled if he had foreseen that it would take him a full 20 years to sell all of the Lido home sites!

Palmer set about selling Lido with enthusiasm. He offered 30-foot inland lots for $700: $440 for the lot and an additional $260 for utilities. Bay front lots were offered at $1800, $1260 plus $540 for utilities. Despite those tempting offers, the economic woes of the Depression left few who could afford to purchase. Undaunted, and instead of reducing prices, Palmer began a campaign to encourage folks to buy not just one lot, but a lot and a half. He told them that they must plan ahead for the many homes that would soon be built on Lido.

Although he was right, many laughed, for homes simply were not being built on Lido Isle, despite Palmer's enthusiasm. One reason was that the Federal Housing Authority (FHA) had not approved Lido for loans, and few had enough ready cash to build without one. Sales finally began to increase when the FHA approved loans for Lido Isle home sites. Immediately, Palmer's marketing campaign went into full swing: He promoted inland 45-foot lots for $1,195 ($100 cash and $10/month) and fine homes for $5000 (at $2.75 a square foot). With 100% financing, he promised that, for as little as $39.48 a month, one could own a prestigious Lido home. He advertised his wonderful deals, using the slogans, *A little buys a lot* and *Lido Isle, a Smart Address*. It soon became a local joke, for Newporters knew that Lido Isle remained little but sand and salt grass.

Not to remain sand and salt grass for long, several other important events helped Lido's transition from a swampy wasteland to the exclusive area it is today:

* The Griffith Company built today's landmark Lido Theatre in 1939.

89

* Also in 1939, a *Life Magazine* crew came to Lido. Its August 21 article, *Life Goes to a Beach Party*, pictured models and starlets swimming, sailing, picnicking, and enjoying themselves on Lido Island. Seen throughout the world, this article gave Lido that glamorous aura it had been seeking ever since it was dredged out of the marshland.

* Tales of buried treasure added just the right touch of mystery to Lido's growing reputation for glamor. While digging an underground utility, workers found an object that was identified as a piece of Spanish gold. An extensive search began, but was stopped suddenly when two searchers were buried and nearly killed. The cessation of the search did nothing to lessen dreams of Spanish treasure on Lido. Although the only buried treasure found was several sacks of high-grade whiskey from rumrunning days, tales of treasure continued to circulate, boosting interest (and sales).

As the 1930s drew to a close, Lido's reputation for exclusive homes was still merely a dream. Nevertheless, the decade had been a good one for Lido Isle. Needed improvements had finally been completed, Palmer had persevered in selling Lido, and national publicity was slowly attracting an interesting, affluent group, ready to participate in Lido Isle's next chapter.

To Washington to Plead Again

By 1933, over $2 million in city and county funds had been spent dredging the channel and building the jetties, but the struggle against silt was far from over. According to **Harry Welch**, Secretary of the Orange County Chamber of Commerce, who began writing a history of Newport Beach several years before his death in 1954, "Up to this time, the amount of money expended on the harbor totaled $2.3 million, but the harbor was like a house without a door."

Despite those expenditures, it was estimated that a daunting $2 million more was needed. Unfortunately, Newporters could not reach

Lido Isle and West Newport in 1940

any deeper into their pockets. Instead, **George Rogers**, a wealthy contractor, whose polio-crippled son had drowned in the entrance, and city engineer **Richard Patterson** went to Washington to plead for federal help one more time. (City coffers were so empty that Rogers paid his own way.)

Harry Welch summarized this 1933 trip to Washington:

> *Folks all over the country were weary, waiting, and worrying. It was a time of deep discouragement—the dark, dreary and dismal days of the 'Depression'. . . . There had been many accidents and cruel, vicious drownings in the Entrance—rip tides that swirled and eddied, 15 and 20 feet high, that caught small craft and hurled them and their human contents, twisted and broken, into the sandy shoals.*

In Washington, they pleaded for funding and spoke poetically of the

91

national advantages of a safe harbor at Newport. They outlined the commercial, military, and recreational advantages of the harbor. According to Welch, they told Washington:

(1) This harbor can be used to relieve the great pressure and congestion existing in such commercial ports as Los Angeles and Long Beach.

(2) The Navy required more space at Los Angeles, and by berthing many of the smaller craft at nearby Newport, the Navy needs would be substantially benefited.

(3) The harbor would be of National benefit in case of war.

(4)[It] would create a harbor refuge for small craft during storms and would stimulate yachting in Southern California.

At long last, Washington listened! After 45 years of unsupportive recommendations by the Army Corps of Engineers, Washington finally approved an allocation to dredge the channel and strengthen its jetties. The approval was made possible by **President Franklin Delano Roosevelt's** New Deal, a plan to combat the Great Depression. An important component of the New Deal was the Works Progress Administration (WPA), designed to get people working again. As a result of WPA, bridges, buildings, and dams were built all over the country. And it was WPA workers who would come to Newport to work on the channel and the jetties. During the darkest days of the Depression, Newporters gleefully celebrated the long-awaited federal funding.

There was a catch to this federal funding: Washington promised to contribute $915,000, if the rest of the estimated cost of $1.83 million could be raised locally. Yet another county bond issue was presented to the debt-burdened voters. Swept by the excitement of the promised federal funding, voters turned a blind eye on their heavy debt burden and approved this bond.

Unfortunately, bureaucratic tangles stopped progress in Washington. Finally, when voters were beginning to think they had been duped into approving a doomed project, Rogers boarded the train for Washington again. Old and ill, he ignored doctor's orders to rest and, instead, lobbied for months until the funding had been restored and progress could continue. Needless to say, Rogers returned home to a hero's welcome for, after almost half a century of rejection, Newport Bay would finally get federal funding.

Work began soon, and, in 15 months, between 8 to 10 million cubic yards of material were dredged from the channel. When complete, the project cost $1.59 million, less than projected, for a welcome change. On May 26, 1936, President Roosevelt pressed a button in Washington that signaled the Navy to signal the Coast Guard, which then transmitted yet another signal to its cutter waiting at the harbor entrance. As soon as this signal was received, a gun was fired, **Governor Frank Merriam** saluted, and a parade of more than 1000 yachts and pleasure boats representing all ports of the Pacific Coast came through the now safe entrance to participate in the on-shore celebration.

Star-studded Times

Already beginning to attract some of the rich and famous with yachts, Newport residents were thrilled when a famous movie star purchased a home. It was big news when James Cagney bought Collins Island, as reported by the *Press-Telegram* on July 7, 1938:

> *One of the largest real estate transfers made here for some time took place yesterday when James Cagney, Hollywood motion picture actor, bought Collins Island from C. A. Price, Arcadia racehorse owner.*
>
> *Cagney, along with Preston Foster, Richard Arlen and other motion picture stars, have been keeping their private yachts here for several years, but Cagney is the first of the top-flight stars to purchase property here.*
>
> *Collins Island is one of the show places in the bay area. It was first built and owned by W. S. Collins, one of the original developers of Balboa Island. Completely surrounded by water with all of the lawn and shrubbery enclosed*

93

within a high wall, the island home is a complete villa with small cottages for guests. Price paid was said to be $45,000.

During those years, the number of Hollywood stars who came to play at Newport significantly increased. Joining James Cagney were **Errol Flynn, Dick Powell, Shirley Temple, Andy Devine, Ray Milland, Buddy Ebsen, Mae West, Humphrey Bogart** and **Lauren Bacall,** and, of course, Newport's favorite, **John Wayne**. They enjoyed yachting in the bay, vacationing at Catalina Island, and playing in Newport's growing number of entertainment spots.

And such entertainment there was! **Madam Osgood**, a local theater owner, brought young women to Balboa to compete in annual beauty contests. Although the contests were popular and well-attended, she had to import girls, for there were not enough local young ladies willing to participate. The landmark Fun Zone also began entertaining folks in 1936, when entrepreneur **Al Anderson**

Fun Zone in 1949

Rendezvous Ballroom

leased land from rancher **Fred Lewis** and began clearing lots for amusement rides and arcades. (Fifty years later, two men, who had worked at the Fun Zone in their youth, formed a corporation to remodel and restore it so that other generations could enjoy its amusements).

When visitors had tired of sailing, swimming, looking for Hollywood stars, watching beauty contests, and enjoying the Fun Zone, such dancing there was! The Balboa Pavilion continued to offer big bands, and was given stiff competition by the new Rendezvous Ballroom, where, once a 50-cent admission charge had been paid, one could dance all night for $1, or pay a nickel for each dance. At those two Balboa ballrooms, couples danced to the music of **Glenn Miller**, the **Dorseys**, **Benny Goodman, Bob Crosby, Lawrence Welk**, and **Stan Kenton.**

Before long, Balboa Peninsula had such a reputation for partying that it was choice of high school and college students from all over the nation for their annual Easter vacation fling. Called Bal Week, it eventually attracted crowds in such high spirits that, by the 1960s, police were forced to impose restrictions that limited its appeal to partyers.

Newport's Transformation

After years of rejection by Washington, it was the administration of Democratic President Franklin D. Roosevelt that finally approved the funds to build a harbor for this Republican-dominated city. The celebratory opening of the harbor and the arrival of movie stars completed Newport's transformation from a locally important playground to a harbor known around the world. At long last, Newport had achieved world-class status for its once-challenged harbor. The positive impact was felt almost immediately as land values increased, and city coffers were replenished by growing tax revenues.

Newport's improved harbor also brought increased numbers of both permanent residents and vacationers to the area. By 1936, it was estimated that the city's population had risen to 3600. There were 2771 homes in the area, 45% of which were owned by year-round residents. Summer and weekend visitors who came to play at the increasingly popular water wonderland owned the other 1522 homes. As a result, the boating and fishing industry thrived, netting an impressive $373,000 in 1933. Despite all of the folks who had come to Newport by this time, there was still plenty of land available for those who wanted to buy—an estimated 12,075 lots were for sale in 1936!

The Depression years brought hardships and victories to Newport. While residents worried about making ends meet and fishing boats lay idle, tenacious Newport leaders were able to convince Washington, at long last, to fund their bay. While Newport's citizens did not completely escape the hardships of the Great Depression, the long-awaited federal funding colored those years in a joyously victorious hue.

World War II Brings Growth, 1939-1959

Newport's business owners anticipated the floods of affluent visitors and homebuyers who would come as soon as the economy improved. But, in 1939, the pier at Newport burned and, fearing that the charred ruin would negatively impact their businesses, they contributed to rebuild it. By June 1940, just in time for the tourist season, the rebuilding was completed, and thousands celebrated its dedication while enjoying a free fish dinner.

As the Depression receded, citizens anticipated that the summer of 1940 would be a highly profitable tourist season. They were right, and they welcomed thousands. They were also delighted when another famous star joined James Cagney in building new summer homes in Newport, as reported in the March 16, 1941 *Press-Telegram:*

> *Permits for the construction of summer homes for Dick Powell and James Cagney, motion picture actors, were issued today. Powell's home will be of six rooms, and cost $7000, and be of wood-frame construction. The Cagney place is to be of five rooms, but of two story, and costing $8500. They will be adjoining improvements at the Bay Shore subdivision just off Coast Highway and the north lagoon channel at Newport Harbor, directly opposite Lido Isle. Both actors are frequent visitors to Newport Beach and Cagney maintains a yacht there.*

Just as more and more were coming to Newport to play, everything changed when Japan attacked Pearl Harbor. Rapidly transitioning from a playground to a military site, Newport was soon occupied with wartime activities.

World War II

The December 7, 1941 attack on Pearl Harbor immediately transformed a disturbing, but distant, European war into a conflict that
threatened Newport's shores. The focus on tourism and leisure
changed to vigilance and preparations for repelling attack. During
the early days of the war, Japanese submarines sank seven U.S. ships
and a pair of unescorted Russian submarines along the West Coast.
Although news of those attacks was censored, and not released until
after the war, Newporters took the potential for attack seriously and
focused their energy on helping to patrol their shores.

Within hours of the Pearl Harbor attack, pleasure boating along the
California coast came to a complete standstill. Newport Harbor was
closed, as were the San Pedro and Wilmington ports. Yachts from
San Pedro and Wilmington were evicted and escorted to Newport,
where they were forced to remain until the war was over. Although
sailing was still permitted inside the bay, the only boats allowed in
and out of Newport were those needed by the military. The Coast
Guard came in force to set up headquarters at Collins Castle. They
placed a barge at the entrance to the bay to check the credentials of
all captains and crews entering or leaving.

Soon after the start of the war, Costa Mesa was selected as the site
of the Santa Ana Army Air Base. The industry Newport had tried
so hard to entice finally came to support the war effort. The South
Coast Company began constructing minesweepers and aircraft rescue boats, while local boatbuilders made cargo carriers, fishing vessels, and a variety of small naval ships. As canneries and fishing
fleets were given priority as wartime industries, Newport's canning
and fishing industries prospered, and wages rose to an impressive
65 cents an hour.

The installations and industries brought military personnel and
workers, all needing housing. For the first time in Newport's history, the demand for housing exceeded the supply. No longer did "For
Sale" and "For Rent" signs dot the landscape. Locals shook their
heads in amazement to find that Newport was full, even in the winter! And, when their work was over for the day, they played. During

98

Warship off Corona del Mar

those years, thousands did the "Balboa Hop" in the Pavilion. They also continued to dance in the Rendezvous Ballroom. The original, built in 1928, had burned in 1935 but was rebuilt and provided a swinging evening out for couples during the war.

Suburban Sprawl

When World War II ended, Newport Beach evolved rapidly, becoming the city we know today. Many servicemen and defense workers returned to Newport. Additionally, automobiles had replaced the Red Cars as the transportation mode of choice, and freeways were beginning to dominate the region. These freeways brought smog to inland valleys, such as San Gabriel, spurring many to move to the clean air on the coast. They also made it easy to commute to Los Angeles from Newport. For the first time, many who had seen Newport as only a weekend getaway began to realize that it could become their home. By the early 1950s, many were surprised to discover that the charming Newport they had fallen in love with had grown to be a vibrant city, boasting a population of over 10,000.

Memorial Day, 1950

During that era of rapid change and before it had cemented its reputation as an expensive and sophisticated place to play and live, Newport Beach was comprised of a wide variety of homes. According to *Southland Magazine* of June 6, 1955:

> *From West Newport to Corona Del Mar is every type of home from modest cottages to sumptuous mansions. Pensioners live in some while others are occupied by such personalities as Johnny Mercer, Ray Milland, and James Cagney.*

Although many who came to buy during those years were of modest means, most soon found that they faced competition from the affluent folks who were also seeking to buy a piece of Newport. Real estate prices for lots that had recently almost been given away rose quickly. Industries, mainly boatbuilders and boat-related services, so recently wooed to the area, were forced to move away to make room for the expensive restaurants, elegant boutiques, and multi-million dollar mansions.

As prices skyrocketed, many were dismayed to discover that they could not find a home they could afford. In a frantic attempt to provide home sites for the willing, moderate-income buyers, entrepreneurial developers acquired more and more surrounding land, and subdivisions such as Bayshores, Cliff Haven, and Linda Isle sprang up. Almost overnight, the lovely surrounding agricultural land disappeared, replaced with affordable housing tracts, shopping centers, and freeways. By 1956, the City of Newport Beach had grown to include 4799 acres of land and 1050 acres of water.

One sign of Newport's transition from a rural town to a modern, efficient city can be seen when a headline-making murder in Newport forced the Sheriff's Department to reorganize so that it could more effectively investigate crime. On March 15, 1947, a yacht explosion in Newport Harbor killed **Walter** and **Beulah Overall,** wealthy Los Angeles residents. Within a few weeks, the Sheriff's Department had uncovered evidence that led them to charge their 17-year-old daughter, **Beulah Louise,** and her boyfriend, **George Gallum**, with the murders. A long, sensational trial followed. By the conclusion, despite the whopping $75,000 bill for evidence analysis, both were acquitted. Frustrated and disappointed, the Sheriff used his failure to get a conviction to lobby successfully for Orange County's own crime lab, in addition to laws controlling the use of explosives.

The Irvine Ranch

The history of the Irvine Ranch is intricately interwoven with the story of Newport. Although James Irvine had acquired the enormous expanse of land, his son, James Irvine II, developed it into one of largest and most productive fruit, grain, and bean ranches in the state. In the 1950s, when people were flooding into the area, the Irvine Company saw an opportunity and began to develop some of its agricultural land.

With the stated purpose of serving the needs of the ever-growing Orange County population, the Irvine Company proceeded to "turn long reaches of lonely water into an ideal resort for all types of pleasure craft [and] to provide miles of homes, bathing beaches, boat anchorages, and yachting basins." As a result, an enormous amount of land surrounding Newport, previously untouchable, was developed into residential tracts. Additionally, the Irvine Company leased land for industrial development to such companies as the Ford Motor Company's Division of Aeronautics and the Collins Radio Company. This radical departure from the historically agricultural mission of the Irvine Family congested the Newport area with even more development.

A succession of Newport's leaders had spent over a century envisioning a vibrant city, strategizing commercial prominence, and enticing folks to buy and build. By the 1960s, it was clear that Newport had emerged as a world-renowned recreational center, home of the wealthy, and a great place to play and spend money. Suddenly, dreams of a flourishing city had been so far exceeded that density and sprawl had emerged as serious concerns. Some were beginning to wonder if Newport's unique small town charm could be retained.

Growth versus Charm, 1960-Present

As Newport Beach entered the last decades of the 20th century, it no longer struggled with being rejected by the federal government, being overshadowed by the Port of Wilmington, or having a landscape dotted with "For Sale" signs. Instead, it had become California's favorite recreational harbor, encircled by expensive homes and wonderful places at which to play and shop. In just a few decades, Newport's struggles shifted from too little (funding, industry, and buyers) to too much (housing, congestion, and noise). Almost overnight, residents had to redirect their energies from promoting their city to protecting it from being consumed by the overwhelming sprawl transforming much of Orange County. And, true to form, residents rose to the challenge of fighting to protect the charming town they loved.

Airport Battles

Their first battle focused on air service to Orange County. A hangar and runway at the future location of Orange County's John Wayne Airport had just been built when World War II began. The army took control of it and added runways and hangars. After the war, the county gained control of the property and, for the next 15 years, a variety of crop dusters, private planes, and Bonanza Airlines used the small airport. They all complained about its inadequate runways. By 1961, it was clear that it was not meeting the rapidly growing urban needs of Orange County, and improvements, totaling $6.3 million, including two more runways and a tower, were recommended.

Opposition from many Orange County residents, especially those of Newport Beach, was strong and loud. Many believe that this issue solidified the series of neighborhoods into a strong, cohesive community voice that demanded attention. Despite the opposition, the expansion was approved and community demands for noise suppression regulations were examined and rejected. By 1967, Orange County had an expanded, refurbished airport. When jets began taking off over Newport Bay, residents knew that their community had changed forever.

By the early 1980s, Newport residents were disappointed to learn that the airport was already inadequate. Orange County was generating 10,000 air passengers daily. John Wayne Airport could accommodate only a small portion of these passengers, and many were forced to use Los Angeles International or Ontario Airports. The Orange County Board of Supervisors, wanting more passengers and airport revenue, announced another expansion. Already inundated with noise, the citizens of Newport rallied to launch another battle. A lawsuit was filed and resulted only in a court-ordered Environmental Impact Report. By 1985, when the report was completed, the expansion was approved. Although agreements were reached that led to history-making noise suppression regulations, Newporters braced for even more deafening noise over their lovely beaches and bay.

Recently, Orange County was again split over an airport issue as a battle raged over the proposed conversion of the El Toro Marine Corps Air Base into Orange County International Airport. In general, Newporters supported the plan with hopes that it would reduce traffic from John Wayne Airport, thus reducing the pervasive aircraft noise. Many southern Orange County residents cited the significantly increased noise pollution and congestion it would generate and mounted a staunch opposition that eventually blocked the development of this proposed new airport. A key theme in Newport Beach for more than four decades, this battle illustrates the ongoing concern with air traffic and its impact on the charm of Newport.

Freeways

Beginning to dominate the Orange County landscape in the 1950s, freeways proliferated during the next few decades. They included the Newport Beach Freeway (CA 55), completed in 1962, the Orange County Freeway (CA 57), completed in 1976, and the

Dory Fleet and Market

Corona del Mar Freeway (CA 73), completed to MacArthur Boulevard in 1979. Although freeway expansion slowed in the 1980s, these freeways provided a convenient transportation corridor that increased the accessibility of Newport Beach and added to its already exploding population. Today, instead of focusing on building more freeways, efforts have shifted toward enhancing steady traffic flow by adding carpool lanes and better access ramps and bridges. Although these efforts have paid off in efficiency, Newport continues to face a host of congestion issues resulting from the complex freeway system.

Newport's Harbor Today

Since the *Vaquero* slowly entered Newport Bay in 1870, the harbor has been the focus of dreams and entrepreneurial schemes for generations of Newport leaders. Although early leaders envisioned a commercial harbor, all would be awed by the lovely bay that emerged from the marshy swampland. While fishing, canning, and shipbuilding coexisted with recreational boating and tourism for many years; during the past few decades, these commercial activities have been supplanted by residential and recreational developement. Today, the focus of the plan for the bay is to retain its special charm and character. Newport's present leaders plan to accomplish this through the support of activities as diverse as recreational and commercial boating, fishing, and swimming; while continuing to support restaurants, retail outlets, parks, nautical museums, and waterfront residential communities. Most would agree that Newport Bay has become one of the most vibrant small boat harbors in the world. No doubt, James MacFadden would have been surprised, but pleased, with what he would see here today.

In the first decade of the 21st century, Newport faces some difficult decisions. Built on the dreams, tenacity, and entrepreneurial spirit of those who saw the promise of its lonely beaches and swampy bay, residents must now balance the development plans of its modern-day visionaries with the importance of retaining its small town charm, wonderful beaches, and world-class recreational harbor.

Cannery, 1970s

Index

A
Edward Abbott 47
Airport 103, 104
Army Corps of Engineers 26, 50, 79, 92

B
Balboa Ferry 57, 62
Balboa Island Improvement Association 62, 68, 71
Joseph Allan Beek 71, 72, 80, 81

C
Juan Rodriguez Cabrillo 5
James Cagney 58, 93, 97
Everett Chance 48
J. Ross Clark 37, 38
William S. Collins 43-45, 55-59, 61
William Clark Crittenden 83, 88

D
Antar Deraga 75
Decree of Secularization 8
Depression 87, 89, 91, 96
Captain Samuel Dunnels 17-19

E
The *Eureka* 29

F
Fire 64
Flint, Bixby, Irvine, and Company 11, 13, 14
Floods 63
Flu 64
Fun Zone 95

G
California Gold Rush 10
Griffith Company 88, 89

H
George Hart 53
Huntington
   Collis 14, 35
   Henry 43, 45
Franz Herding 83
Colonel W. H. Holabird 37
The *Humboldt* 8

I
Irvines 15, 18, 19, 22-24, 30, 36, 39, 53, 67, 102

K
Duke Kahanamoku 74, 77-78

L
Little Aggie 81

M

Glenn Martin 59, 60
McFaddens 13, 15, 16,
    19-40, 106
Sam and Vera Meyers 52
Missions 5, 6
Helena Modjeska 54, 55
George Morales 64
Movies 59, 74
The *Muriel* 75, 76

N

Native Americans 6, 7, 11
The *Newport* 21-23
Newport News 52, 64

O

Walter and Beulah Overall 101

P

Paul Palmer 89
W. K. Parkinson 82, 84
Pavilion 7, 46, 48, 95
Juan Pablo Peralta 6, 9, 11, 14
Gaspar de Portola 5

R

Railroads 16, 22, 25, 31-40, 42
Ranchos 8-11, 13, 15

Red Cars 43, 45, 46, 48, 49, 53
Rendezvous Ballroom 80, 95
Dr. Conrad Richter 65
George Rogers 91, 93
Franklin D. Roosevelt 92, 95

S

Rufus Sanborn 53
Santa Ana River 7, 11, 63, 64, 66
Jose Sepulveda 9-11

T

The *Thelma* 77
Title Insurance and Trust of
    Los Angeles 88, 89
Stephen Townsend 44

V

The *Vaquero* 16-19

W

Captain John Watts 57
Wharf 27-40
Wilson Brothers 20

Y

Jose Antonio Yorba 6, 9, 11, 14